How The Righteous Suffer

a commentary on Job
(Second Edition)

David B. Caton

for
Samantha

CONTENTS

PREFACE

This is the second edition of *How The Righteous Suffer*. I have written a few more books this one and I thought some changes were appropriate, particularly adding a chapter about Eliphaz, Bildad and Zophar and their implications related to false prophecy/teaching today. I have also added significantly to the chapter, *How to Portray Satan*. The original conclusion has not changed but my understanding of this evil personality has. A few minor issues related to headings has been remedied also.

Surprise was the most common response I received when I told people that this, my latest project, was a commentary on the book of Job. I imagine that the thought behind the surprise was, "Why spend so much time on an obscure book of the Bible?" And some people voiced words to that effect. It would seem that the book of Job does not readily come in on the 'top 10' list of Christians' favourite books of the Bible. This is quite understandable; it is long, often confusing, appears repetitive and superficially there appears to be no clear point. The narrative is short and therefore might not be considered a good read, the poetry goes on and on, it is easy to confuse who is saying what and perhaps even more difficult to decide is what is truth and what is not. In short, for many, the book of Job is a book left alone…

Notwithstanding, since the first edition has been published some people have told me that Job is indeed their favourite book of the Bible. However, the initial concerns, which I have heard over the years is precisely the reason for writing this commentary. Notwithstanding that there are many fine commentaries on this book, however, most Christians do not read commentaries. That statement, of course, begs the question, why, then, would anyone read yours? It is my hope that this commentary will be read alongside the Bible text and with the mostly short explanations given, will help the reader gain a clearer understanding of what each speaker is saying and the motive behind what is said. Where my commentary is different from others, in my attempt at least, is to simply open the book in such a way that the reader can glean the precious truths that are contained within as it is read devotionally.

I comment on the prologue in such a way as to give the reader the background to the drama both on earth and in heaven. Following each section of the speeches I give a one sentence summary indicating the main point the speaker is making. Following that, I give a paragraph (or two) to further elaborate the point being made. The epilogue is treated in the same fashion.

For me, the great theme of the book of Job is how the righteous suffer. Job's question is always why, but that question is never answered by God and Job becomes an example for us in terms of how to suffer, particularly when there appears to be no good reason for it because the sufferer has been living righteously before God. His righteousness is borne out by God's comment to Ezekiel where Job is placed alongside two other men of righteous faith, Noah and Daniel (Eze 14:14, 20); Job has much to teach us which is confirmed in James (5:11). Through this book we learn of God's sovereign majesty, His mercy, His loving kindness toward His whole creation, and His willingness to forgive and enable the imprudent to not remain estranged from Him. While it is entitled the *Book of Job*, and the man plays a central role, Almighty God is the central character and it is toward God and His self-revelation that all the lessons point. We also learn how a person in difficult circumstances ought to carry themselves before their Creator. We learn from Job through what he did well and not so well. Much also can be learned from his friends and they can be viewed as examples of how the church, at times, fails to understand and minister to those who are suffering under the hand of God.

I envision the reader of this commentary, with their favourite version of the Bible by their side, reading the Bible text and then the comment for the appropriate section. It is my hope and prayer that the wonderful truths that God has to share with his children through this story will be illuminated with the ultimate result being a greater adoration and submission to the One who created and cares so deeply for His creation, and like Job, discover where true wisdom is to be found.

I would like to give thanks to God for His gentle guidance and to my wife, Vivian, who has spent much time reading and re-reading the proof with me. Also much thanks is extended to our brother and friend, Craig, who came on board with this project and gave much help.

David B. Caton

HOW THE RIGHTEOUS SUFFER

Job's story reflects the stories of many people in one specific aspect that is disheartening for so many; he never receives an answer to his burning question. The specific circumstances that surround the question that people ask will vary, but in almost all cases the issue of 'why' will be at the forefront, and in most instances the question will never be answered. How a person responds to the lack of answer is critical to their future. The absence of an adequate answer can leave a person permanently cynical, permanently patient and anything in between. The big 'why' question usually centres around personal suffering and as a general rule people are naturally averse to suffering. It is far from an ideal state and yet there are overwhelming numbers of people who currently suffer around the world and have done so throughout the ages; where there is death there is often suffering. This would indicate that suffering is indeed a natural state for humanity. Yet despite the overwhelming evidence of this fact of global suffering, few believe it to be ideal and wish to throw off its rigours and this is certainly true for many people who claim Christian faith.

There are two seemingly competing messages in the Bible: one is peace and material prosperity, the rewards of obedience to God, and the other is living with suffering, which also is found in the same place as peace and prosperity—obedience, and both are possible for the follower of Christ as the writer of Hebrews takes pains to point out (Heb 11).

In the story of Job, helpfully, we see both at work. The drama opens with an idyllic pastoral scene where Job's great wealth and piety is described; added to this is God's commendation upon him. Unknown to Job is the heavenly drama and he finds himself quickly thrust from his idyllic life into one of unimaginable torment— the man loses everything a man can lose except for his life (and wife). Within the community in which he was once honoured, he becomes completely isolated; he is a pariah. Those who had been previously jealous of him gloated over his misfortune and those who made a living on the back of his prosperity were resentful. In their minds there is only one person to blame for their loss and that was Job. God must be punishing him because of his hypocrisy—he was not the righteous man he presented as, at best he was a secret sinner.

As Job sits in the ash heap of the communal rubbish dump he is visited by four of his friends who hope to comfort him. Their desire, as it transpires, is to bring Job to repentance in order to find God's forgiveness and the restoration of his fortunes. This was commendable because their motivation was for Job's restoration. However, in order to achieve that restoration, they believe that Job needs to heed their good advice. This Job could not do because in doing so he has to admit that he is something that he knew he is not.

All four of Job's friends believed that God was

punishing Job because of his wickedness. They never knew exactly of what his wickedness entailed, but his suffering circumstances was proof enough to them that he must have been wicked. As a result, no matter how much Job protested his innocence they would not be dissuaded from their belief—reinforced by the evidence of their own eyes. To them their conclusion had to be correct because it fitted hand in glove with their assumptions. While they tested Job's veracity, they never attempted the same with regard to their assumptions.

Naturally, Job gained no comfort from his friends and he turns his attention toward God. He desperately wants his suffering to end, but that is not his primary focus when questioning God. At the forefront of Job's mind is the question 'why'. Job's question was essentially, "Why am I, a righteous man, devoted to God, suffering like the wicked ought to suffer?" To which his friends responded, "That's because you're wicked." Job knew that he wasn't and so too, the reader of the story. From the prologue the reader knows that God has allowed Satan to torment Job in such a complete fashion that for Job, his only hope becomes death and that hope was denied. However, being aware of the drama in the heavenly council, the reader goes no further in finding an adequate explanation as to why God allowed His favoured servant to suffer in this way. Thus Job and the reader are in the same position.

The reader becomes aware by the end of the story that through Job's righteousness the *Accuser* is defeated and God proves His majesty. What might not be so clear to the reader is that God had placed Himself on trial as a result of Satan presumptuously declaring Job's self-centred motive in piety and has proved Himself to be true, triumphing morally over evil through Job. Therefore, Job, in part, has suffered as a result of God's vindication of him against Satan's accusation and thus Job's suffering is not to humiliate him, but rather, the *Accuser*. And yet, knowing that still does not answer fully why it was necessary for a loving God, favourably disposed toward such a worthy man, to take him through such agony. Without an adequate answer the perceptive reader ought to consider an alternative question.

Job finally has his time in court with God. He has prepared his case and is certain that when it is presented, God will relent (13:18; 23:4). However, even though Job is afforded the opportunity to speak he finds that his previous words, which were many, in actual fact were ignorant and empty. He admits that there is more to existence than that of which he is cognisant. His big question vanishes and he accepts and submits to God's sovereign right to do as He wills without scrutiny from His creation, all-the-while trusting that God has his best interests at heart. For the creature created in God's image, still bearing the marks of 'the fall', this kind of surrender is no easy journey. The place of complete trust in God seems a destination easy to get to and in which to reside when all things are going well, as it was for Job before his great calamity. It is entirely another matter, however, to trust God and believe in His personal loving kindness when our circumstances are in tatters—and to discover our trust in God was not nearly as deep as we might have thought it was. If a life could be compared with a vibrant city, Job's might be compared to Coventry, Dresden, Stalingrad or Warsaw just prior to World War Two; prosperous, full of life and, superficially at least, carefree. But following the ravages of war these cities were bleak, not even a shadow of their former selves. Life could hardly be sustained, only eked out among the rubble of buildings and the suffering of the people.[1] This was Job and in this devastated state he was expected to find hope, comfort and loving kindness in the God he worshiped despite the destruction, not only around him, but on him and in him. We might pray that God would not take us to such extremes. However, Job did find God's comfort, not after his fortunes were restored, but while still on the ash pile (42:6). The word repent בֶּחָם (nāham) also carries the meaning 'to comfort'. Thus, through this encounter with God, Job has seen afresh his God's sovereign majesty, understood that there was much he did not comprehend nor could comprehend with regard to the intricacies of life, and though still suffering, he has been comforted. Job can trust his God without being dependant on external prosperity. The faith that he had in God prior to this great calamity, while shaken to its

---

[1] At the time of writing, one might compare the Syrian cities of Aleppo and Homs in a similar way (sadly, still true when writing the second edition).

core, never crumbled, and has subsequently been revitalised and, arguably, placed on a better foundation—all without his question being answered.

The question must change as the people of faith orientate themselves toward God being more fully the central figure as opposed to their own person being the object of divine orbit. Psychologist and author Dr. James Dobson wrote a helpful book about the issue of suffering, *When God Doesn't Make Sense.*[2] In his book he sums up with the need for 'tough faith' and cites positive examples both biblical and post biblical. He is without doubt right, however, in these days I believe God would take us a step further on this journey as He did with Job. James Dobson's title speaks from a human perspective, when God doesn't make sense to us. I believe the Spirit of God is urging Christ's church to instead look more from God's perspective. Job's central focus initially was on himself and God did not make sense to him anymore. In the end, though, his focus was no longer upon himself and he simply trusted— still in the ashes, with blackened and weeping skin and with the eyes of men condemning. I do not wish such suffering on anybody, but pray that God would lead His people out of self-centred folly into Christo-centric righteousness that can trust God in all circumstances as Jesus demonstrated before going to the cross (Jn 14:28-31).

Therefore, the question changes from why do the

---

[2] J. Dobson, *When God Doesn't Make Sense,* (Wheaton, Illinois: Tyndale, 1993).

righteous suffer, to how do the righteous suffer? The 'why' will often remain in the inexplicable will of God and thus the fact of suffering is no reason to not believe—the justification many give for walking away from the faith. The created can certainly ask questions of their Creator and Jesus has made a way to the Father for all who believe and they can, therefore, come before Him with confidence (cf. Heb 10:19ff.). However, we cannot put God on trial as Job wished, nor can we demand answers; while God is responsible for His creation, He is in no way responsible to it. That is not to say that a person of faith ought not ask the question 'why', but it is to say that if no answer is forthcoming, that ought to be accepted with a continual trust in the benevolence of God. If the righteous in Christ can accept suffering as part of God's will for their lives, for whatever length of time God determines, they can then look to God for comfort in that suffering (cf. Ps 23:4) and seek Him as to how to walk with Him through it.

For the first three hundred years of the church, suffering in the form of persecution under Roman rule was a regular feature. Suffering began with Jesus and has continued throughout the church age. Not every devout believer has suffered terribly; some have lived exceedingly blessed and prosperous lives, however, it would seem that such people are in the minority. According to David Barrett and Todd Johnson, authors of *World Christian Trends AD30-AD2200*, at the time of writing the annual number of Christian martyrs was

160,000 with that trend set to increase.[3] For the number of martyrs, there are many more that have to live with insult and mistreatment in various forms[4] as well as Christians who suffer trials in life without a seeming direct correlation to their faith. God certainly allows this, Jesus said it would happen (cf. Mt 10:22; Mk 13:13; Lk 21:17; Jn 15:18ff.), but why it has to be this way is a divine mystery. The church can appreciate Satan's attack upon God and all that God loves, even how wicked men would want to stamp out righteousness, but why God allows this to be so is another matter altogether. The church must accept that this is the will of God and trust Him to bring His dearly loved people through it into eternity. This is no recipe for fatalism, however. The church has been given a mission in the face of opposition, which bears the love and grace of the One who gave the mission (Mt 28:18-20), and to those members who are suffering the church is charged with comfort and care (cf. Mt 25:31ff.).

If it can be accepted that suffering can fall upon the righteous and, as it was with Job, for no other reason than his righteousness, I trust it also can be accepted that the sufferer can trust that God knows what He is doing and that the reason as to why will not always be forthcoming. If the aforementioned can be accepted,

---

[3] See David Barrett and Todd Johnson, *World Christian Trends AD30-AD2200,* (Pasadena: William Carey Library, 2001), 229.
[4] For an excellent analysis of persecution against the church, see Roland Boyd-Macmillan, *Faith That Endures – The Essential Guide to the Persecuted Church,* (Lancaster: Sovereign World, 2006).

then we need to discuss how the righteous suffer. For the answer to this we ought to look at Peter's first epistle. He is writing to the suffering church and offers the appropriate Christian attitude in the face of suffering, giving an incisive instruction: *"So then, those who suffer according to God's will should commit themselves to their faithful Creator and continue to do good." (1Pe 4:19 NIV).* The 'way of righteousness' is to be walked no matter what life's circumstances.

Job had clearly walked 'the way of righteousness' before his suffering. Satan accused him before God stating that the only reason for his piety was God's protection and prosperity (1:9-10). God of course knew Job and knew that his worship was founded on something far deeper than external blessing, something which Satan could not see. Therefore, God allowed Satan certain rights over his life which culminated in Job's misery. Satan believed that Job would curse God (1:11; 2:5) in his pitiful state, but as God knew all along, Job would not. Job was perplexed, in anguish, his theology turned upside down and he demanded God tell him why. Yet, despite his torment he never turned from God, even though he believed that God's harsh treatment was needless. His worship of God was founded on the fact that God is,[5] and no matter how much he suffered, that would not change. He knew,

---

[5] God said to Moses, "I am who I am" (Ex 3:14). This title is connected with the verb 'to be' (is) and relates to God's pre-existent, all powerful nature.

consequently, that fearing the Lord was wisdom and rejecting evil was understanding (28:28) and his suffering did not change any of that, therefore he held onto his integrity and it was to God alone he looked for his vindication.

There is a triumphalist aspect to the gospel message and it would be wrong to encourage Christians to simply expect suffering in this life; Job's suffering was only temporary. However, the Christian triumph is only completed with the return of Christ. From the eternal perspective, in this life, both prosperity and poverty are temporary conditions. There are certainly temptations associated with prosperity, however, these are seldom the concern for most Christians (perhaps they ought to be), nor is this the issue with which the 'world' takes the church to task. The world will ask, "If God is so loving, why is there so much evil?" To which the church seldom offers an adequate explanation and to which the 'world' does not really want an answer; just another reason to justify unbelief. But just as God exists, so too suffering and through it He has purpose. Sadly, so much suffering comes through the hands of people, as did much of Job's. A life submitted to God would do no such thing; sadly, a life partially submitted to God might. Therefore, the righteous who suffer must look to God and continue to do what is right before Him, to whom they are ultimately answerable. Job's life was one of triumph; he triumphed in his prosperity and in his poverty. For the Christian, triumph is Christ's life remaining within no matter what our circumstances.

Job's friends came to comfort him and become for us an object lesson of what not to do. They diagnosed the cause and delivered an appropriate prognosis, however, the diagnosis was incorrect. Had Job followed their well-meaning advice, he would have been worse off. If we should find ourselves in the fortunate position of not suffering, it becomes incumbent upon us to render comfort to those who are (Gal 6:10) without presuming the antecedents to suffering if they are not clear. We often simply do not have answers, but we can offer comfort (2Co 1:3ff.) and help carry another's burden; the rest remains with God whom we seek.

Despite the fact that suffering is all around us, we tend to live in denial of it and are often perplexed when trials come upon us. Sometimes the cause is obvious and sometimes not. For the Christian the response ought to always be the same: we humbly submit to His purposes, seek Him for the cause and deliverance, wait patiently for His vindication and continue to walk faithfully before Him. That is how the righteous suffer; the lesson from Job, the teaching of Jesus and the apostles. Certainly not an easy lesson to learn, but as the apostle Paul affirmed for his own life, we too can do this as God gives us strength (Phil 4:12).

HOW TO PORTRAY SATAN

When commenting on the book of Job one must consider the author's framework: the intended audience, the author's theology, worldview and approach to the Old Testament in general, and so on. The archetypical protagonist, Satan, poses some issues within that framework. The question that needs answering is, "How should Satan be portrayed?" It is easy for a modern Christian reading the book of Job to simply apply a Christian theological approach to this evil character, which is supported by the way English Bibles translate שָׂטָן (śātān) in the Old Testament. In the book of Job and in Zechariah (3:1, 2), the word Satan always has the definite article preceding it, i.e. הַשָּׂטָן (haśātān), 'the' Satan, and not as two separate words. Therefore, the Hebrew text is using the term as a designation *(the accuser)*, while English translations use the term as a proper noun (Satan). The latter denotes personality, the former function. The English translations are being consistent with New Testament rendering where Satan is used as a proper noun, as when Jesus speaks to Satan (Mt 4:10), but records Jesus going into the desert to be tempted by the devil, (Mt 4:1), that is, the slanderer or accuser; same meaning but denoting function. However, whether this usual interpretation ought to be applied to the Old Testament when that understanding had not been developed is another matter altogether. It could be argued that translators in these instances have moved beyond translation and are in fact indulging in interpretation.[6]

The personality and role of Satan in Hebraic thought began to be more fully developed during the time of exile in Babylon. Thus, the writer of Chronicles (possibly Ezra) writing some 60 or 70 years after Zechariah records that David was enticed by Satan to take a census (1Ch 21:1). In this instance, and the last time Satan is mentioned in the Old Testament canon (chronologically), his name is without the definite article and so naturally Satan becomes the accuser's name—named for what he is.

During the intertestamental period (c. 400 BC-1 AD) Satan's persona was significantly developed and was given a number of names such as Azazel (1 Enoch 13:1), Beelzeboul (Testament of Solomon 6), Belial (1QS 2:19 [Dead Sea Scrolls, Manual of Discipline]), or Beliar (Jubilees 1:20), the devil (Wisdom of Solomon 2:24), among others. Names such as Belial, Beelzebub and the devil were used by the New Testament writers, including Jesus Himself (cf. Mt 10:25; 12:27; 13:39; 25:41; Lk 8:12; 11:18, 19; Jn 8:44). As a result, these names had to be used in reformed translations despite the

---

[6] Whether Jerome (*Eusebius Sophronius Hieronymus* [Saint Jerome] c. 347-420 AD) was the first to use the interpretation of Satan's personhood in Job when he produced the Vulgate (published c. 405 AD) cannot be certain, however, the tradition of interpreting Satan in this way rather than translating what the text says has continued throughout church history, to the author's knowledge, without exception.

Protestant aversion to the Apocrypha and Pseudepigrapha. Thus, by the 1st century, Jesus made it clear who the enemy really is (Jn 8:44). The epistles develop the understanding of the supernatural battle (1Pe 5:8) in which Satan leads the evil host (Rev 12:9) and with which the church is in constant struggle (Eph 6:12), and through Christ's help, will overcome (Rev 20:10). If the book of Job is a story set during the time of the Patriarchs, then neither the writer nor early readers would have carried such nuanced ideas about Satan. He is not mentioned by any of the human characters in the drama either, although a frightening spiritual presence is referenced by Eliphaz (Job 4:15), which could have been the devil himself, but that is not explored any further. This is, of course, one of the arguments for the story being much younger.

In the New Testament the Greek use of the proper noun Satan Σατανᾶς is essentially a Greek transliteration of the Hebrew. In Greek thought there was no direct parallel within their pantheon. Jewish apocalyptic thinking during the intertestamental period understood Satan's function and limitations to be in submission to the sovereign God and are consistent with New Testament teaching. Thus there is no appropriation from Hellenistic thought which permeated the known world in the first century AD.

While there have been influences upon Hebraic thought with regard to Satan's identity and purpose, it is difficult to see the New Testament's understanding in parallel with other ideas even Persian Zoroastrianism, to which the Jewish exiles and diaspora would have been exposed. The concepts of Satan or the devil today, whether accurate or not, would be drawn from the New Testament rather than being pre-existent in evangelised cultures. Thus, the adversary concept in a person (spiritual being) is biblical and not borrowed. The fact that within the contemporary world that the concept the devil or Satan exists in almost every culture is as a result of evangelism and the spread of the word of God, rather than pre-existing conceptions.

When speaking of Satan in terms of function the New Testament writers use the term διάβολος, 'the devil', which is how the Septuagint translators translated *'the satan'* into Greek, as its root meaning is accuse. In the New Testament, then, we find both persona and function clearly identified in one being and translators have, perhaps understandably, but not accurately, used the proper noun in Job.

My intended audience is Christians who do not necessarily have interpretive training, nor desire any and could consider, in my opinion, that such more accurate nuances add little to the message. Therefore, in this commentary I have chosen to use 'Satan' as a proper noun, a personal spiritual being, rather than as a designation. To use the term 'the Satan' would, I think, be awkward for readers. I have to then confess that this commentary is laced with evangelical Christian interpretation and my conception of 'the Satan' in the book of Job is that of the personality at war with God and His people, and who has always, since the creation of man at least, been at war with God and His people, still subject to God's sovereign will. Many scholars would disagree with this approach and I can understand their reasoning, but for this commentary I think it is the better approach as the activity of the character *'the satan'* in the book of Job is entirely consistent with the New Testament presentation of him: a murderer and a liar (Jn 8:44).

THE STORY OF JOB

The book of Job begins with an introduction to the central human character, Job, who is described as an extremely prosperous man. He is also devout and worships the one true God in all faithfulness and acts as a priest on behalf of his family. It is his faithful devotion to God and his subsequent blameless life that causes Job to be the object of scrutiny in the heavenly council. When the sons of God gather, the reader is given a glimpse into the heavenly realms and consequently understands, at a superficial level, the antecedents to Job's suffering. God draws the accuser's (Satan) attention to blameless and upright Job. Satan has surely studied Job and asserts that his piety is founded in gratefulness for God's protection and prosperity and suggests that if prosperity is withdrawn Job would then revert to cursing God. Satan clearly understands something of human nature. God, therefore, allows Satan the control of all that belongs to Job, the only proviso is that Job, himself, is not to be harmed—clearly Satan's desire is to harm. His considered and vicious response to God's licence is to destroy Job's wealth and children. Satan may have some understanding of human behaviour, but that understanding is wrongly applied to Job. The man does not curse God and maintains a steadfast commitment. The human characters in this story are oblivious to this heavenly drama and when Job's friends try to solve the puzzling cause of his suffering this crucial incident will never feature in their considerations, and determining a truthful conclusion without all the facts is a lottery.

The scene following the attack on Job's prosperity is a return to the heavenly council where God, again, draws Satan's attention to Job and his blameless and upright nature. To be clear, this second scene ensures there is no doubt as to who is the instigator of Job's suffering, and in actual fact who is the central character to the story—God. Essentially God is saying, "Satan, you were wrong. Job's devotion has nothing to do with the hedge of protection or prosperity that I had given him." Satan responds by accusing human beings of having far more base motivations than that; in fact, suggesting that human beings are willing to give up all in order to save their lives or avoid suffering physically (a position it would appear he still firmly holds). God allows Satan the authority to harm Job physically, but not to kill him, without giving any justification. Immediately, as if Satan has already considered his next step and is prepared, he inflicts painful sores upon the whole of Job's body; these sores neither worsen nor improve. This leaves Job in abject misery and yet, contrary to Satan's prediction, he still will not curse God, even at the behest of his wife (2:9), but retains his devotion.

Satan does not appear in the drama again and his influence and significance in the drama ought not be overestimated—he is merely an actor performing in accordance with God's sovereign will. Not, though, as a marionette, but with volition under the superintendence of an all-knowing, all-seeing God.

The reader next observes the subsequent events played out on earth as the human characters seek to understand what has happened and offer counsel as to how the situation might be remedied. Eliphaz, Bildad and Zophar share the same simple theological assumption—that suffering comes from the hand of God and is God's punishment on evildoers. Their conclusion, therefore, is that Job is a sinner, not upright and blameless (as God has stated) but is self-deluded, and because they cannot convince Job of this he is, therefore, without hope—the worst of sinners. The fourth friend, and last to speak, Elihu, goes a step further theologically and suggests that the suffering that God inflicts on the wicked is His way of bringing a person to repentance and thus restoration. Therefore, Elihu's conclusion is that God's infliction of suffering on an unrighteous Job is an act of mercy. He also cannot convince Job of his need to repent and concludes as the others have, that Job suffers from an intolerable case of self-righteousness and is a hopeless case, again the worst of sinners. The two arguments that Job's friends make contain an element of truth to them, but the reader is aware that their assumptions regarding the initiation of Job's suffering are foundationally wrong and therefore, so must be their advice.

Thus Job finds no comfort from his friends and looks to God. He continually pleads for his day in the heavenly court that he might question God as to His motives for making him needlessly suffer. Job believes that if he were to present his case, God would see His error in Job's suffering and relent. This perhaps gives some insight into Job's need for theological development. Job's assumption is that God has made a mistake. His friends would argue that God has not, and in this case, they were correct, but for the wrong reasons. As a result of the different theological assumptions, interpretations of Job's experience and the conclusions that are drawn Job and his friends could never come to a place of common understanding and thus his friends could not provide any comfort for him, even though that was their expressed intention.

Job, indeed, has his day in court, but it is not as he expects. Faced with the awesome majesty, power and wisdom of God, Job discovers that he has no place within the created order to question God's motives. God instead questions Job, which invites him to reconsider the mystery and complexity and often sheer unfathomableness of the world that God has created in which Job had been placed. Job, and the reader also, is to understand that the moral order is comparable to the natural order of the universe. Much of it remains beyond human comprehension, and some of what can be comprehended seems hideous, futile, or fearsome, but all of it is the work of a wise God who has made the world the way it is for His own purposes.[7] Job's suffering belongs here—in the humanly unfathomable. The picture God creates for Job by His questioning is altogether different to the ordered universe Job had previously envisioned, and arguably is still at odds with how most Christians envision it. Therefore, the distance between human and the divine understanding is too great and Job finds that his only response can be to repent—the lesson for the church—ignorance being no excuse.

Repentance is what Elihu prescribed, the necessary response for Job's supposed wickedness in order to come back into God's favour. Instead, Job's repentance comes as a result of his discovery, through God's questions, that the knowledge on which he built his case for demanding an audience with God is seriously insufficient. Job's accusation that God was wrong in bringing suffering upon him had no place and put the man, as it does with all humanity in the face of divine Judgement, powerless, insufficient and in desperate need of mercy. In the end Job concludes that he did not know what he was talking about, which, ironically was one of the accusations that his friends made against him, however, those accusations were based on different assumptions.

Throughout the various dialogues Job was far

---

[7]For an excellent summary of the purpose of God's speech to Job see, David Clines, 'Job', *New International Bible Commentary on CD-ROM*, (Grand Rapids: Zondervan, nd.), comment 38:1-42:6.

closer to the truth than were his companions. Basically, Job was righteous, as righteous as man subject to the fall might be, and was suffering as a righteous man. His friends, however, concluded that Job was suffering as a result of God's judgement on a wicked man. As a result of their wrong assumptions these friends have not spoken wrongly of Job alone, but more seriously of God. God is angry with them; the folly of their words was serious and they were to be judged accordingly. The size of the offering that God commanded indicated just how serious speaking wrongly of Him is. It was to Job, the one they had accused of being unrighteous, they had to present the offerings and he would then act as their priest—a further vindication of Job. God may have been angry with Eliphaz, Bildad and Zophar's 'wicked words' however, He offered mercy and would forgive their foolish talk if they followed the prescribed ritual. God's concern and grace in this story is not limited to Job.

Inherent in the priestly act is God elevating Job in the eyes of his companions and reinforcing the point that they were wrong in their assumptions, and subsequent assessment. God then restores Job's fortunes to a greater measure than before the disaster that befell him, and thus Job lives a full life (a further 140 years) restored of blessing, wealth and honour. The restoration proved to a theologically inept community that Job was indeed a righteous man. Satan's assumptions are also proven to be entirely wrong when applied to Job. Other men might curse God when suffering under such devastating circumstances, but clearly Satan did not know all men as God did (or does). This is the central issue to the story underscoring God's omniscience. Thus, God's moral universe continues unmarred despite the heavenly and human drama. Job's lesson, and that for the reader too, is that God knows all and can be trusted, and is to be trusted despite human suppositions arguing to the contrary. Suffering in this life cannot always easily be defined in a cause and effect argument and so in this too the faithful ought to keep their trust in God. Therefore, whether good or ill is received in life, the message of Job speaks clearly; "The fear of the Lord—that is wisdom, and to shun evil is understanding." (28:28).

COMMENTARY

Prologue

1:1

The book of Job begins with an introduction to the central human character. Job lived in the land of Uz. Little is known about the location. It could well have been east of the Jordon. In God's dialogue with Job the Jordon river is mentioned in such a way that the reader would assume Job has some knowledge of the river (40:23). Uz is also mentioned in Jeremiah (25:20) in conjunction with the nations that will receive punishment from God, and in Lamentations (4:21) where the daughters of Edom will live.

The dating of the book is problematic and the events could have occurred anywhere from the time of the Patriarchs to the time of the Judges. There is no indication that Job or his friends are Israelites, but they do worship God. There is no mention of the Law or tabernacle worship but while the absence of any of these cannot be used to draw any concrete conclusion, it would appear that the setting takes place before the conquest of the land and Job's long life (42:16) is a possible clue for this setting.

Job is described by the author as blameless and upright (v. 1) and this description is confirmed by God (v. 8). His lifestyle was such that he rejected evil and feared God. The evil he rejected was evil from God's perspective, and apart from the Law, Job and his friends had an intimate knowledge of right and wrong from God's perspective.

1:2-3

Job is described as the complete man; not only is he righteous and blameless he has great prosperity. He has ten children; seven sons and three daughters, a sign of the blessing of God. His ownership of his livestock is linked together in order to show complete blessing; seven thousand sheep, three thousand camels—ten thousand combined. The large number of camels indicates his ability to trade over long distances. Five hundred yoke of oxen, צֶמֶד (*semed*) yoke, a team of two, or a pair; this can also refer to a measurement of land, as the acreage a team of animals can plough. The number of oxen indicates that Job was capable of tilling a large area of land and presumably owned a considerable quantity of land. The NIV lists Job with five hundred donkeys; these are אָתוֹן (*'ātōn*) female donkeys, valuable for their foals and milk and of more value than male donkeys. Job is also described as owning a large number of slaves; another sign of his great wealth. Even Abraham was not described as being as prosperous as Job. The number of livestock and the subsequent number of people needed to work them would indicate that there were sufficient numbers of people attached to Job that a town centred around him with many people being dependent upon his great fortune. In his time of great trial, not only did his children suffer (their lives taken), but the many people dependent upon Job would have lost much also. Job later compares the treatment (by men) he received before his suffering and afterward (ch. 29-30) indicating the dependency many had on him and reflects people's often unkind reaction when they lose their source of provision, even perhaps the jealousy that people often feel toward the successful, which sometimes becomes delight when that success is lost.

As the text reads, Job was the greatest man among all the people of the East in terms of both wealth and social status. The inference is that this great wealth was the blessing of God due to his great piety.

1:4-5

Job acted as a priest to his family, which was traditionally the role of the head. Clearly this was more than a ritual function for Job; he was truly concerned for his children's standing before God. As with any festive activity where drinking alcohol is a focus[8] there is the strong possibility, as alcohol subdues inhibition, that sin will be committed. Job, therefore, acts as a mediator between God and his children. However, Job is not simply concerned for any outward or behavioural sins but also for the inward sins that people might commit against God in a state of intoxication or revelry. Therefore, he diligently offered sacrifices on behalf of his children in case they had cursed God in their hearts. It is interesting to note that

---

[8] מִשְׁתֶּה (*mišteh*), a feast or banquet, with a focus on drinking.

the text indicates that Job did not attend the feasts arranged by his children.

1:6

The scene in this drama shifts from the introduction of Job to the heavenly council where the sons of god בְּנֵי־ הָאֱלֹהִים (NIV angels) presented themselves before God as did Satan. There is no apparent discrepancy with this as the text reads; Satan was acting in accordance with his created status, however, the sense of antagonism is evident from the beginning. The name Satan, שָׂטָן can mean (human) adversary, accuser, one who opposes, slanderer. Used as a proper noun, Satan is the spirit being who is an opponent of God and slanderer of His creation. He apparently has access to the heavenly council despite his opposition to all that is of God and continues to have activities in the heavenly realms (Eph 6:12). He operates using deception—about himself, his purpose, his activities, and his coming defeat (Rev 12:9). Satan mentioned here, could well be the personal being of evil found in Christian theology, but at the time of writing the character of Satan in Hebrew theology is not that well defined.

1:7

Satan has not been idle; he spends his time roaming throughout the earth. The sense of the text is that he has sinister intent; looking for failings in people in order to accuse them before God. God's questioning of Satan does not mean that we are to assume God's ignorance of Satan's activities, but rather in order to illicit a response to which God already knows the answer.

1:8

As Satan has said, he has been roaming throughout the earth; presumably his focus has been on human beings. God narrows his focus upon one figure, who, given Satan's response he has also observed, and Job is isolated as being unique in piety. God boasts about Job and uses the same phrase as the narrator (v. 1), according Job the honour of being His servant; as with Abraham, Moses, David and Isaiah. Job being non-Jewish indicates, as with Nebuchadnezzar (Jer 25:9), that even at this point in redemptive history God had not limited Himself and purposes to the Abrahamic family alone.

1:9-11

Satan dismisses Job's disinterested piety as Job's obligated response because of God's favour upon him—giving him protection and prosperity. Satan is suggesting that Job's upright character is hypocritical and not innate. He hypothesizes that if God were to take away all that He has given Job, then Job would turn on God and curse Him. However, Satan does not use the word curse אָרַר (*’ārar*), instead he uses בָּרַךְ (*bārak*) which is 'to bless'; indicating the intense sarcasm with which Satan addresses God.

Inherent in the prologue is the idea that Job's prosperity is directly attributed to his piety (1:2). Satan has voiced his accusation, but it is still an assumption. With the heavenly council observing this dialogue presumably they, too, would like to know. The test that Satan proposes is not to show that prosperity is the motive for Job's piety, but rather, because in Job's case prosperity and piety are so intertwined, that prosperity needs to be removed to see the relationship between the two. It is interesting to note God's warning to the Israelites through Moses in relation to prosperity (Dt 6:12; 8:11). The fear there is the opposite of the situation with Job; that with the Israelites, prosperity will cause impiety. Presumably Satan is well aware of this and his questioning has deeper motives than the superficial assertion of Job's self-interest.

1:12

How is the reader supposed to interpret this verse in relation to the purposes of God? An early Hebraic reader would most certainly read into it something very different from a modern Christian with a developed theology of the sovereignty of God. The story-line suggests that God does not know the outcome and though He has confidence in Job, He too, along with the heavenly council, is interested to know the outcome. Is God, in His sovereignty, using Job to prove Himself right against one of His subordinates; in which case Job is simply a pawn for the 'gods' to move and create drama on earth, perhaps simply for their own entertainment? Whether God, in His omniscience, has confidence in Job and wants to prove Job righteous against Satan's accusation or even if God is allowing this situation to further refine Job, the answer is never forthcoming and leaves the interpreter with only speculation. What is certainly clear in the verse is that God is in control and Satan can only afflict as God allows. Whether Job has an understanding of the personality Satan or not the reader can never know, but in all his trials his questions are to God whom Job firmly believes is the perpetrator of his sufferings; and that is how the story is to be read. Delegated permission is delegated authority and therefore, the one who delegates bears the ultimate responsibility.

Satan leaves the heavenly council. There is no suggestion that he left quickly to perform his acts of evil against Job as v. 13 begins, "One day". The reader can be forgiven if they sense the tantalizing effect this permission has on Satan. It is as if, having left the presence of God, he goes to plan how best to afflict God's servant in the most complete and devastating way possible. Satan wants to be proven right as well.

1:13

The scene changes from heavenly council to earth with no hint in the following drama that heaven is involved. The attacks are both human and natural in form; Sabeans come from the South (Sheba), the Chaldeans from the north, violent thunderstorms (from the Palestinian perspective) come from the west and a whirlwind from the desert in the east. Attacks from raiding parties were not unknown in the ancient world, nor natural events such as thunderstorms and whirlwinds. However, the devastating nature of the natural disasters indicates that they are at the very least preternatural[9] and given the permission God has given to Satan the reader could view them as supernatural. The effect being that with each increasing blow everything Job has, his immense wealth and those he considers dear to him are destroyed in a single day.

Calamity falls in a well-planned and co-ordinated four-fronted attack in quick succession bringing blow upon blow from all corners of the compass in the most demoralising fashion upon Job. The day begins as tranquil as any day—people are going about their usual business (v. 14); the proverbial calm before the storm. Job's children are feasting as was their custom (1:4); this is almost antithetical to the run of the next few verses. It gives the reader a sense that perhaps Job's fears were correct that in their feasting they may have been cursing God (1:5) as this is the precursor to the following attacks. This sets the scene of a day beginning like any other, where unknown to the central earthly characters great disaster has been carefully planned and is about to befall the unsuspecting family.

1:14-15

A messenger comes to Job informing him of the disaster that has befallen his oxen and donkeys at the hands of Sabeans (from present day Yemen). If

---

[9] That is, beyond what is considered to be normal in nature.

plunder had been the only motive for the Sabean attack it is unlikely that they would have put all but one to the sword. This detail highlights the dramatic necessity (on Satan's part) to eliminate all of Job's possessions.

1:16

While the first messenger is still speaking, another comes to Job and informs him of a further disaster; this time not at the hands of men, but of nature. The phrase 'fire from God' indicates that this is no usual fire, even more dramatic than the fire and lightning as part of the seventh plague (Ex 9:23) for it consumes seven thousand sheep and their attending shepherds. This continues the theme of the total elimination of Job's possessions.

1:17

The second messenger is speaking and a third now arrives with bad news. The Chaldeans, probably nomadic peoples of southern Mesopotamia, who are known to have lived there as early as the tenth century BC,[10] engage in a co-ordinated attack. They form three parties and take Job's three thousand camels,[11] killing

---

[10] Clines, David J. A., *Word Biblical Commentary : Job 1-20 on CD-ROM*, (Dallas : Word, 2002), comment 1:17.

[11] It might be too long a reach to suggest that all of Job's camels were together at this time. Camels' primary use would have been for trade and many could well possibly have been journeying to or from their home base at the time of the attack. Nevertheless the completeness of Job's loss is envisioned here.

the attendants, as with the shepherds before.

1:18-19

A fourth messenger appears while the third is still speaking and repeats the narrator's opening to the calamities (1:13); Job's sons and daughters are eating and feasting. As if out of nowhere a wind (tornado) from the east destroys Job's eldest son's house and all who are in it, save one. Whirlwinds or tornados are a rare, but not unknown occurrence.[12] However, this is a preternatural event as all four corners of the house are struck. The number four speaks of complete ruin as in Eze 14:12–23. God sends a four-pronged judgement due to Israel's unfaithfulness using famine, wild beasts, the sword, and plague (c.f. also the four horns of Zec 2:1-4 [1:18-21]; the four horsemen of the apocalypse (Rev 6:1-18) and four angels of Rev 9:13-15; and the seven calamities of Job 5:19).

Job's obvious love and concern for his children is evident from the beginning of the narrative and this is the crescendo of the disasters. The objective of his priestly function was to ensure their right standing with God and perhaps to have their standing and prosperity continue, but now, despite his priestly intercession, the human legacy of Job is destroyed. What does Job have if he does not have his children? In a culture where children take care of the welfare of the aged parent they are an economic necessity; this last

---

[12] Clines cites tornados and whirlwinds in Israel in the winters of 1954-55 and 1955-56. See Clines, *Job 1-20*, comment 1:18-19.

blow is truly the one that takes all that Job has.

1:20

With no time for these calamities to really sink in; in utter shock and in terrible grief we see the true heart of Job's attitude to his possessions; even his children. To tear one's outer garment and crop one's hair were common gestures of violent grief in the biblical world. Such a response to grief included weeping and wailing (Ps 42:3; Jn 11:33-35).

Job is absolutely grief stricken. With no way of knowing what has transpired in the heavenly council and that these calamities have come from the hand of Satan, Job rightly attributes his loss directly to God. At the point of this acknowledgement is the question of how Job will respond. To have anything simply taken from us is considered a violation and injustice, and perhaps if it was just the Sabeans or the Chaldeans who had taken some of Job's livestock then Job may have mounted a party to get them back as Abram did for his nephew Lot (Ge 14:1-16) or David did in Ziklag (1Sa 30:1-20). But, for Job, this was complete loss and his choice is to either curse God, as was Satan's taunt, or to worship. Job responds by worshiping God; thus proving Satan wrong regarding Job's inherent attitude. Sarcastically Satan said that Job will bless בָּרַךְ (*bārak*) God and it is the very thing that Job does in this case, not in sarcasm, but in genuine sincerity (cf. 2:3).

1:21

Job voices his worship in a pessimistic form of

wisdom that speaks of the inevitability of death. The beginning and the end occur in similar fashion; a person begins with nothing and finishes with nothing. Job, perhaps at this crucial point, considers his life to be extremely close to its end. His phrasing of his beginning and end is paralleled in Psalm 139, where verse 13 speaks of an individual's creation in the mother's womb, and verse 15 of that same individual's creation in the depths of the earth. It is the intervening years on which Job focuses his concern; he has had much, which has come from the Lord's hand and now the Lord יְהוָה (Yahweh) has taken. May the name of Yahweh be praised בָּרַךְ (*bārak*) [bless]. Job does not at this point, nor at any other say God has given and the Sabeans, the lightning, the Chaldeans or whirlwind has taken; these are only secondary causes. It is not so much in the giving or the taking for which Yahweh is to be praised by Job, but rather for who God is to Job.

1:22

The implication is that if Job had cursed or charged God with wrongdoing that would have been counted as a sin and Job's response marks the high point of the drama. This shows quite a different attitude to the dialogue that follows; not that Job sins in the dialogue, but in the darkness of his despair he is not content to allow a serene compliant submission to his God who can give and take and reign supreme because the fabric of his belief has now been turned upside down and he wants answers in relation to the doctrine of retribution. But Job's initial response to this part of the test is to continue with his unceasing reverence toward God. At the very end of the drama this constant reverence toward his God is even more certain.

2:1

There is no indication of how much time has elapsed from the day of Job's calamities to this fourth scene of the drama. On another day, the sons of God present themselves before God. Here the repetition begins following the second scene. Satan comes along with the sons of God and presents himself before the Lord (Yahweh).

2:2

The Lord asks the same question as in 1:7 with the same pretended naivety. The question could be paralleled to a parent about to confront a child over an issue and asking, "What have you been doing?" when, all along, the parent knows full well. God addresses the same type of question to Cain 4:6, 8 when God knew exactly the source of Cain's morose behaviour and what had become of Abel. Satan gives the same casual response as in 1:7. Satan's assumption regarding Job's piety has been proven wrong and therefore he cannot come into God's presence in order to gloat. Perhaps Satan might be prepared to make no more of the issue; he was wrong and in his pride he certainly would not want to draw attention to the fact. It is God again who initiates the focus upon Job.

2:3

Ignoring what had transpired in their previous encounter and initially, at least, ignoring the consequences, God asks Satan to consider His servant, Job. As if nothing has happened God continues describing Job as a unique person who is blameless and upright—a man who fears God and shuns evil. Satan knows full well what has happened to Job and despite the great tragedy that Satan so willingly afflicted upon him, Job's status before God has not changed.

Then God shifts from the repetition of the previous encounter and adds that Job still maintains his integrity, saying that though you (Satan) incited me against him to ruin him without any reason. This is the sting in the tail of God's supposed naivety. Not only has Job maintained חָזַק (*ḥāzaq*) his integrity, this wording indicates that he has been strengthened by it as if to say his resolve is stronger than ever.

God says that Satan incited Him without reason חִנָּם (*hinnām*). The doctrine of retribution is undone at this point; there is no clear cause and effect based on Job's behaviour. Clearly there is cause and effect as the gods observe humanity and intervene at will as in Greek and Roman mythology. But in view throughout the book of Job is the human conception that God is not capricious or whimsical, but is the holder of the universe in order, enabling human beings to live their lives with a sense of security and not terror. The story of Job demonstrates that bad things can happen to good/righteous people and whether good or ill is received in life ought not have any bearing on our attitudes toward worship. However, we are not to read this as if Satan stirred God up to allow something that was against His will. Though Job (and the reader) never receive an answer for the cause of the suffering, it was God's inscrutable will that Job should suffer.

2:4-6

Satan has not given up on his quest to be proven right. He has observed Job's reactions to his attacks (1:21) and so has God. Satan's response to God is so immediate and emphatic it suggests that he has been considering what ought to be the next step if he were given the chance. "Skin for skin" is his response. The exact meaning of this proverbial saying is unclear, however, Satan's intent is undoubtedly clear; he believes that a man will give up everything in order to keep his own life. Presumably Satan has witnessed this himself, as he has roamed the earth. This is an idea that is expressed in contemporary society through the media of television and movies and not without good reason. However, it is not an absolute truth and while many will give up everything in order to spare their own lives there are many out of principle and conviction who will not. Inherent in that response is choice—Job, however, is not in such a position—he is given no choice. Therefore, the idea being presented is what Job will do if he now loses his health. Will he hold tenaciously onto the life he is given at all costs? Job is given no choice of health or even death. The question is entirely whether or not Job, having been afflicted in his body, after losing all else and now losing his health, with such a level of affliction that he will even despair of life, where he feels the breath of death, but not actually dying (or even being allowed to die, but wishing for it), will he now curse God? Satan, of course, assumes that he will—supposedly even wants him to in order to prove himself right over God and thus continue his attack upon God.

Again, as it was with the first attack upon Job, we see Satan limited in his power. It is God who ultimately allows this to happen as Satan has no possessive rights over Job who is God's servant (so too Satan). The proverbial saying, "If you've got your health you've got everything" is the type of sentiment that Satan is using and God has not allowed him to take that from Job—now his 'everything' will be taken. As in 1:11-12 Satan will act as God's agent; the "hand" that is "put forth" against Job is Yahweh's, and at the same time the "hand" which will smite Job is Satan's.

2:7

In this last scene there is no sense of Satan biding his time as in 1:13. He immediately goes out and afflicts Job's body with painful sores. Painful sores (NIV) שְׁחִין (šᵉhîn) is a general term that could be used to describe various skin diseases; there is no way of knowing the precise diagnosis, but most likely running sores, perhaps boils. What is clear is that this affliction carried out by Satan is debilitating; one that would cause the afflicted to wish for death and curse God for the misery that He has allowed without the relief of death, which is, of course, Satan's intention. At various points in his dialogue, Job describes his symptoms; his body is clothed with worms and scabs, with broken and festering skin (7:5), his skin turns black and peels and he burns with fever (30:30). As a consequence of his affliction Job has lost his body weight (19:20) and presumably along with that much of his strength. The ongoing effects also include nightmares (7:14), sleeplessness (7:4) and weeping (16:16) and, therefore, Job is more than physically afflicted, but also psychologically.

2:8

Job sits among the ashes; this is quite likely to be the public town rubbish heap. According to David Clines, the sense of the Hebrew is that Job's presence in the ashes is not as a result of the affliction of sores, but that Job was already there in mourning from the first attack.[13] In his isolation and displacement from all he once knew he picks up pieces of pottery to scrape his skin, which may be itching and oozing pus—portraying a man in utter destitution.

2:9

Entering into this desperate scene is Job's wife. It would seem more than coincidental that her advice to Job is the very accusation of Satan. This is a further temptation for Job and must further exacerbate his mental anguish. Her question, "Are you still holding

---

[13] Clines, *Job 1-20*, comment 2:8.

onto your integrity?", and her subsequent advice, "Curse God and die", casts her into the role of Satan's real or unwitting assistant. From her perspective, through no fault of her own, she has lost everything along with Job. There is no suggestion from the text as to why she has been spared and the fact that she does not suffer as Job indicates, from man's perspective at least, that she is an innocent party and any guilt or shame that is borne upon Job is hers only by association. Her question and advice suggests that she, too, believes that Job's prosperity was the direct result of his piety. Without his prosperity and viz-a-viz, hers too, why should he fear God for nothing?

This is a significant issue for the contemporary church. God as divine benefactor is presented as the basis of much evangelism; coupled with living a victorious life is God's willingness to prosper the faithful. There is, of course, much truth to this, but it can and does fall into the category of overemphasised truth or even heterodoxy. Christians may well believe in a glorious life after death with Christ, but for so many that is not nearly enough to maintain an allegiance with God. When disaster strikes, (and Jesus never promised a life free from troubles [John 16:33]) the disaster does not fit the conception of a God who solves all personal problems or ensures a smooth ride in life. The phrase, "I tried Christianity, but it didn't work for me," or something similar is often heard. At the centre of Job's wife's concerns, and for many in church, is 'self'. It would seem then, that the central reason for worshiping God is the benefits received and disinterested piety, as in Job's case, is still a rare commodity.

2:10

Job, like Adam was tempted by his wife. Unlike Adam, Job did not accept his wife's advice. David Clines, based on his translation, suggests that Job is referring to a *group* of foolish women as he rebukes his wife, and what Job is implying is thus; "You talk like a low-class, irreligious woman; such words are beneath you."[14] This draws away from the often thought sense that Job's wife is perhaps superficial and vain, but instead as a woman of standing with aristocratic hauteur, in keeping with the story's world, the lower classes were considered to be less religious, therefore, such talk was out of place for Job's wife. What is remarkable is how Job responds to his wife and to his situation. He does not accuse his wife of blasphemy, but responds to her as though she has spoken out of desperation and not of her usual self.

Job continues with his idealism in relation to his worship of God; God is worshiped. There is no reason to not worship and at this point Satan is undone. For Job the worship of God is now proven not to be found in the supposed accompanying benefits and this is more than God taking a neutral stand in the affairs of man. If God blesses it is natural to worship, but Job will worship God even if God chooses to do him harm. Job reiterates this idea in 13:15 and the same sentiment

---

[14]Clines, *Job 1-20*, comment 2:9.

can be seen with Shadrach, Meshach and Abednego as they are threatened with Nebuchadnezzar's furnace (Da 3:18). Like the three friends of Daniel, Job trusts his God. There is no sense here of a well-defined theology, but a man responding to circumstances never experienced before and declaring what is in his heart. Jesus made the statement much later (Mt 12:34) that the mouth speaks what is in the heart and Job's heart is truly revealed at this point.

The narrator continues that Job did not sin in what he said. Had he cursed God for his troubles that would have been sin for him and what Satan had predicted (2:5). However, it does foreshadow the far darker way in which Job expresses himself as he begins his dialogue in 3:1. Up to this point Job is accepting of God's right to give and take, but later the narrative is turned to Job questioning the reason for his suffering and his desperation for answers. It is not uncommon for a person to philosophically accept calamity initially, but as the person has time to reflect, and especially if their circumstances do not improve, that philosophical acceptance turns to questioning, doubt, grievance and even anger or loss of faith. In Job's case there is no loss of faith, his attention is always turned toward God who, Job affirms, is the architect of his suffering and to whom he poses the eternal question, "Why?"

2:11

The scene changes again with the introduction of Job's friends: Eliphaz, king of Teman, Bildad, the ruler of the Shuhites, and Zophar king of the Minaeans (see Septuagint). They have come to comfort him in his time of trouble. They are ignorant of the course of events that occurred in the council of heaven that have led to Job's suffering, but will comment on what has transpired with Job. Perhaps some weeks or even months have passed since Job's calamities. It would take some time for word to have reached his friends and still further time for them to organise themselves to arrive together. They come with good intentions in order to comfort נָחַם (*nāham*); this word bears two distinct but related meanings in the Old Testament; to comfort or console, and to relent, repent, change one's mind and be grieved.[15] It would seem that Job's friends came with the former and after hearing Job, sought the latter.

2:12-13

Upon seeing Job they are distressed and from a distance they struggle to recognise him; not that they do not know it is Job, but more that the reality is worse than the reports they have heard. They immediately join Job in a drastic form of mourning reserved for death or total disaster. This could be seen as a foreshadowing of their future dialogue as tormentors and not comforters as they treat him as if already dead, however, more likely it is a sincere attempt to identify

---

[15] William D. Mounce, *Mounce's Complete Expository Dictionary of Old and New Testament Words,* (Grand Rapids: Zondervan, 2006), 122.

with their friend's grief. These men would have been as eminent in their locations as Job was in his and thus it was their noble robes they tore, and they threw dust up into the air as they sat in silence. For one of them to speak before the sufferer would not be the correct etiquette and perhaps in their silence they reflected on the reasons for Job's suffering to which later they would give voice in their comfort נָחַם (*nāham*) in order for Job to repent.

The speeches of these three friends will not reach to the heart of Job's distress, and he criticises them sharply for this (cf. 13:4). Their fault lies in their uncritical acceptance of orthodox theology and their inability to see that Job's is a special case. In this the question of why suffering occurs is addressed, though not resolved, and thus the heart of the issue becomes what should the innocent do when inexplicable suffering comes upon them? Thus the book of Job is not a theoretical book about the issue of innocent suffering to which no satisfactory answer is given, but a practical book of how to behave before a sovereign, unseen, Almighty God who is the author of all the events that transpire on the earth.

Job's complaint (3:1-26)

Job breaks the silence which now links the previous narrative to the present poetry. Satan's accusation was that Job would curse God (1:11; 2:5) and is so encouraged by his wife (2:9). In the catastrophes poured out on Job the narrator presents him in humble pious submission, willing to accept all that has come from God's hand. As Job's monologue begins we find a distinct change of mood, however; instead of cursing God, Job curses the day he was born. This is not the sarcastic tone of the devil (1:11; 2:5) בָּרַךְ (*bārak*), but קִלֵּל (*qālal*); to curse with the sense of despising his life. At this point we see the pious humanity of Job rather than the pious philosophical Job. He has had further time to reflect on his sufferings. Previously as he sat in the ash heap he was alone, but in the last seven days he has been joined by his three friends who have mourned with him, though not speaking.

In the presence of his friends Job begins to speak, though he does not address them but instead verbalises his internal reflection. It is a common human response to calamity to wish one had never been born; the sentiment expressed this way as the sufferer sees little or no hope of undoing their present circumstance which outweighs any previous good in life. In Job's case too, the memories of the good days of the past cannot soothe his now miserable soul.

It is interesting to note throughout this initial monologue and Job's subsequent responses, that while he wishes he had never been born or even that his God would take his life (6:8-9), nowhere does Job contemplate suicide. Presumably even then suicide was considered to be a sinful act, inappropriate for the pious man despite such miserable circumstances. Perhaps not just because of the sin factor, but also, and maybe even more importantly, is the hope that Job still has in God (13:15). Even though Job despairs of his life, he has not despaired of all hope as he clearly sees his life wrapped in his God (cf. 19:25ff.) It would appear that in all of his suffering Job has not completely lost heart; he has come close to it, but his tenacious hold upon God means that, despairing as he is, he is able to continue to look beyond himself. The apostle Paul echoes such a sentiment (2 Co 4:16-18) as he encourages the Corinthian Christians to look beyond the natural in the face of troubles, and look to God in whom are the promises of a better future. Never losing sight of God is Job's very present anchor and also true in the new covenant for all who would claim allegiance to Christ.

3:1-19

Job begins with cursing the day of his birth, now that he is suffering life is not worth living.

Job's world has been shattered; his ordered and pious life which helped keep his world balanced has been turned upside down. In his first monologue Job's focus is not so much on the anguish of his physical suffering or even the loss of family and possessions that might be the most shattering for him, rather the loss of the sense of moral order on which he has built his life. He claims his innocence, but later his friends will also claim and assert Job's lack of innocence. Here at this point of his suffering Job prefers the order of Sheol, the order of inactivity, rather than the chaos through which he is living. He is not blaming God for this, but longs for God to release him from it.

3:20-26

Job questions why light is given to a man who has no future, so that even death becomes, in comparison, a treasure; Job has feared that this might happen to him.

To what extent Job has previously feared these events (3:25) and to what conclusions he has come cannot be clear. Certainly in the prologue the reader is told of the man who was fearful that his children may have sinned and cursed God in their hearts (1:5) for which he made appropriate sacrifice. Did Job see a direct relationship between his and his family's prosperity and his piety? This could be so even if Job is disinterested. Job would worship God under any circumstances, but as the future discussions reveal all the human actors in this drama believe in the law of retribution. Perhaps Job may have a heart toward God, but blessing and prosperity from obedience is clearly presented from Genesis on (see Abraham—Ge 12:1-2; 22:15-17; Isaac—Ge 26:2-3) and into the New Testament where the faithful in Christ receive the same promises (Gal 3:16-18, 26-28). Job believed that such blessing could be lost and whoever he might have blamed (not himself) we can never know, but we do know that he had feared the possibility. The irony is that his loss was not as a result of sin, his or anyone else's, but because of his righteousness, a critical fact of which the reader is aware, but Job and his friends are not.

Eliphaz the Temanite's First Speech (4:1-5:27)

Eliphaz was a man from Teman, an Edomite city noted as a centre of wisdom (Jer 49:7). The Septuagint records him as being a king (2:11). He is the eldest of Job's comforters, tradition being that the eldest speaks first. His influence is clearly seen on Bildad and Zophar.

On the surface he spoke as if he thought Job was basically righteous and that his sufferings were temporary. He appealed, as a point of reference, to a revelation that came to him from the voice of a spirit that had spoken to him at night (4:12ff.). The spirit put forth a question that became a fundamental issue for Eliphaz, "Can a mortal be more righteous than God?" Frustrated that Job would not heed his advice, Eliphaz would later voice his concern that Job was not so righteous.

4:1-6

Eliphaz begins his speech by trying to refocus Job on the success of his past.

After the days of mourning Eliphaz speaks. He has come to comfort Job, but now after Job's speech he seeks to answer Job's question. He tells Job to find hope in the good works of the past (v. 6). The belief being that Job's sufferings were a temporary condition and his righteous past will be rewarded with God's visible favour again. Eliphaz speaks as the representative of a broad consensus within the wisdom tradition: the 'fear of God' is the principal part of wisdom (Prov 1:7). It is the chief requirement for anyone who would live well and long since life is the aim of wisdom.[16] This, of course, does not speak to why Job has suffered at this point and Eliphaz's position is a clear case of a man's theology not giving any allowance for another's reality. Eliphaz believes that Job has no grounds for confidence due to his piety because of the desperate circumstances he faces, to which Eliphaz speaks of another reality.

4:7-11

Eliphaz begins to cast doubt on Job's good name.

After initially asserting Job's blameless תֹם (*tōm*) name Eliphaz begins to cast doubt on it, the premise being that bad things happen to bad people (v. 7). He may have implied that Job ought not suffer the fate of the wicked, but the fact that Job is suffering belies such a confidence. Eliphaz can see it and can therefore be of no comfort to Job.

4:12-21

Eliphaz describes an encounter with a spirit who gives him revelation and this forms the basis for his

---

[16] Clines, *Job 1-20*, comment, 4:6.

arguments against Job.

Eliphaz describes an encounter of the night with a spirit רוּחַ (*rūah*). רוּחַ (*rūah*) has a wide range of meanings such as 'wind' or 'breath', it can be used to describe the general character of a group, supernatural or angelic beings, including the Spirit of God. The question is, who spoke to Eliphaz? This is an important question because the inferences that Eliphaz draws from what he hears forms the foundations of his assumptions about Job and later God declares to Eliphaz that he had not spoken about God with a correct understanding (42:7). It would, therefore, seem unlikely that the entity that he encountered was in fact the Spirit of God; perhaps even Satan himself. The message Eliphaz receives is a mixture of truth and lie and places great emphasis on the insignificance of human life, unnoticed by God (4:20). Jesus makes the opposite claim (Mt 10:29-31) announcing that even the hairs of a person's head are counted by God. The seeds of doubt relating to God's goodness are posed by the spirit's question and perhaps the most telling statement that God charges his angels with error (4:18b) gives the reader a clue to the identity or allegiance of this spirit. Who speaks the truth has been the issue between God and Satan from the beginning, and as Job failed to fulfil Satan's expectation Satan is clearly in error, but perhaps still unwilling to concede, which begs the question; to what extent are Job's friends unwitting assistants of Satan as Job's wife may have been? The effect of their 'comfort' is to take Job into deep despair and although there is no further hint of Satan's involvement there is no reason to rule the possibility out.

Revealed to Eliphaz is the idea that God's angels are not entirely trustworthy (v. 18) and if that is the case then so too human beings (those who live in houses of clay) [v19]. The inference here is that although Job has been confirmed as righteous by Eliphaz he cannot possibly be perfect and therefore some suffering might be due to come upon him.

5:1-7

Eliphaz reflects that inherent with man's life is trouble.

Eliphaz recounts his reflections on life. Job cannot call upon one of the holy ones because, according to Eliphaz, they too are far from God (4:18). He has seen that a man breeds trouble for himself (v7). The fool אֱוִיל (*'ewîl*) is not simply the unwise, but the purposefully unrighteous and Eliphaz has seen such people begin to prosper, but their prosperity never lasts; in the end what they labour for is taken from them. This supports his idea that the wicked are punished and the righteous rewarded, nevertheless, trouble is an unavoidable part of a man's life according to Eliphaz.

5:8-16

Eliphaz advises Job to appeal to God.

It is not to holy ones or angels that Job should appeal (v. 1); not that Job ever made such a suggestion. Eliphaz advises that Job should appeal to God who is sovereign over nature and thwarts the plans of the crafty עָרוּם (*ʿārûm*). A modern term could be the 'street smart'; people who deftly derive good incomes from less than honest means. God also rescues those in need (often from the crafty). Eliphaz contends that God is the great reverser of fortunes (vv. 11-16) and, therefore, Job ought to appeal to God for the reversal of his.

5:17-26

According to Eliphaz, correction from God is a beneficial experience and therefore it should be accepted because yielding to it will bring prosperity to life.

Eliphaz, at this point, is inferring that Job is suffering only temporary punishment from God. Job is advised not to despise the discipline of the Almighty and then all things will come back to Job; his financial prosperity and family. It is possible to imagine the restoration of Job's material losses, but his family? This must have been difficult for Job to hear and a particularly insensitive comment (v. 25) for Eliphaz to make.

Another inference that can be drawn from Eliphaz's comment, which will become explicit later, is that Job is not as righteous as he has made out, otherwise there would be no need of punishment. Despite Eliphaz's promise of better days they are of no consequence to Job because the premise on which they are built, that is, Job's punishment for wickedness, is incorrect.

5:27

Eliphaz tells Job to apply his advice.

The wisdom tradition to which Eliphaz belongs has a clear understanding of the diagnosis and the necessary prognosis for Job. He is clearly closed to any different possibility as to the cause of Job's suffering and to Eliphaz Job's inquiry as to why he is suffering is a waste of time when, in Eliphaz's mind, the reasons are quite clear. Job, however, cannot condescend to Eliphaz's wisdom because that would force him to deny his integrity, which he, rightly, holds onto throughout the discourse. However, like so many who give advice, Eliphaz's expectation is that it should be heeded believing that having done so God will restore.

Job's Second Speech (6:1-7:21)

6:1-7

Job feels compelled to cry out because his misery is so great, asserting that this is a natural thing to do.

Job acknowledges that he has vented his feelings in an impetuous לַעַע (*lā'a'*) or impulsive manner. In his defence he asserts that this is the most natural thing to do as the Almighty שַׁדַּי (*šadday*), a common title for

God in Job, has laid such overwhelming misery upon him. Using natural examples; wild donkey, the ox, he emphasises that when a creature has its basic needs met it does not complain. The implication being, then neither would Job. If food can be taken as a metaphor (v. 6) then Eliphaz's words to Job provide no comfort at all and he rejects them completely.

6:8-10

In order to relieve Job of his great distress Job wants God to take his life while he has still maintained his integrity and not denied God.

At this point of Job's dialogue, the reader is given a sense of just how important the issue of not denying God is to Job and that the very real fear he has is that, in his despair, he just might. Job's request for death is not simply for the nightmare in which he lives to end, but more importantly, that his life would end while he still remains true to God.

6:11-13

Job sees no need to be patient (particularly in waiting for death) as he has lost all hope for the future.

Eliphaz spoke of Job's success (4:2-6) and Job's response here is that success has been driven from him, therefore, he now has no natural ability, a further aspect of life taken from him. Life for Job now carries little value and death is to be preferred before he succumbs to cursing God.

6:14-23

Job is greatly disappointed in his friends whom he likens to a stream that flows in the cooler seasons but dries up when it is most needed (summer) because, rather than supporting him, they have found fault with him.

Job's sad indictment upon his friends is most pointed in v. 21. The example he gives of what he has found in his friends is the same as the hope afforded by a known water supply when, after travelling long distances one finds that it no longer exists and thus the hope becomes bitter disappointment; even death is more comfort to Job than his friends now. He has asked nothing of them materially, only supporting friendship, but instead they have found fault with him. They (certainly Eliphaz) at this point cannot see beyond their theological assumptions, which the reader, and Job, know to be incorrect. As right and sincere as Job's friends might think they are, they are sincerely wrong.

6:24:27

Job feels his friends have no regard for him or his words.

Job has been plunged into further despair by the counsel of his friends. Such is the resentment that he feels that he suggests that they are as heartless as a person who would sell an orphan into slavery or sell a friend as a mere commodity. There is no suggestion that Job's friends have actually done such things and perhaps the analogy is not particularly apt, but Job's comment does reveal the deep anguish he feels as a result of the disappointment with his friends.

6:28-30

Job pleads for his friends to reassess their conclusions because his very integrity is at stake.

Job reaffirms the honesty of his own words and using a softer tone asks his friends to reconsider their assessment of him. As a loyal friend to a loyal friend, he pleads his innocence in the hope that they will accept his words and believe him. Job has nothing left in life except his integrity before God and it would seem to Job that his friends are attempting to take even that away. Minus the support of his friends, Job stands truly alone and it is alone before God that he makes his appeal and alone before God he will later stand.

7:1-5

As Job reflects on the harshness of life and the futile aspirations of the slave and hired worker, he sees himself in the same vein made worse by the agony of long sleepless nights and the painful putrid flesh of his body.

Such is Job's suffering that his life can only be considered in the present; his past life is over, though it could hardly be considered 'hard service' (that is not to say he didn't work hard). Now he sees himself as burdened as any common man. His hope at this point, too, is as futile as the slave's because his only hope is death. The terrible skin condition is a constant torment; it never gets worse, which would probably bring death, but it doesn't get better either. Job is forced to remain in a constant state of misery.

7:6-10

Job now begins to address God directly, requesting that God would remember him before his anticipated death.

On one hand Job speaks of the slowness of the night (v. 4) and on the other the speed of his life, which he believes is coming to a premature end. This is no real contradiction, but simply his response to two pressing aspects of his life; one, the immediacy of the agony of sleepless nights with nothing to do in the darkness but to wait for the morning light. The other is the reflection upon his life as a whole and to realise how quickly life has passed now that he faces death as a result of his incurable disease. Job's response is to address God directly; his friends (certainly Eliphaz up to this point) have been of no comfort, therefore, he has no other recourse, except to speak to God.

Job wants God to remember him (v. 7). According to David Clines, remembering in this context implies that God's concentration is elsewhere, and that, if God, the one to whom Job has been praying, would even for a moment take note of the fact of Job's overwhelmingly obvious condition, He would immediately set about changing the situation.[17] However, Job is not convinced that God will look upon him again, certainly not with the favour he would like and the only outcome that Job can possibly see is his non-existence, when not even God will be able to see him.

Though he has begged for death (6:9) as a release from his suffering, it can be inferred from this passage that that is not Job's first choice. He wants to see happiness again (v. 7), but his fear is that God will not remember him and that is the only place his hope rests. Therefore, if he can't have life, and in his miserable condition Job cannot consider his existence as having anything in the way of 'quality of life', there is but one other alternative—death, which can only be seen as the hope of a desperate man.

7:11-16

As a result of only having death as his hope, Job develops the fortitude to complain to God about the misery God has brought upon him.

The righteous Job, who has held onto his integrity and will not curse God takes a step further into venting his despair by complaining to God. This would not have been an easy thing for Job to do and Job's bitterness of soul (v. 11) gives him licence to take this step. The present question uppermost in Job's mind is why does God keep him corralled for torture?

---

[17]Clines, *Job 1-20*, comment 7:7.

Obviously Job does not think God has forgotten him (v. 7) outright, but certainly forgotten that he is a man who deserves to be blessed. However, even when Job does get to sleep his torment continues, for which he blames God, but the reader knows that this is a vicious relentless attack upon a man in whom God delights. Therefore, without meaning or purpose, with only misery and torment, life is of little value to Job and he wants God to leave him alone so that he can die.

7:17-21

Job begins to be more explicit in questioning God as to why God should target him specifically and leave him in this misery, especially when there appears no purpose in it.

Job begins his next thought with what many commentators call a parody of Psalm 8:5-6. Such a comment is dependent on the dating of the book but it is certainly possible that this type of phrasing, "What is man that you make so much of him..." was coined before the psalmist penned his words. God makes so much of man because man is the creation of God in His own image and whose purpose for the world centres in man, His crowning creation,[18] to whom He has given the world. However, at this point in Job's suffering, all Job can see is that God's only interest in him is to torment him for any possible sins that he may

---

[18] Elmer B. Smick, 'Job', *Zondervan NIV Bible Commentary on CD-ROM*, (Grand Rapids: Zondervan, nd.), comment 7:11-21.

have committed.

Job's suggestion to God is that if God might forgive his sins this would, in Job's mind, release him from his torment. The rationale behind such a suggestion is Job's assertion that he will soon die (v. 21) and then he will be of no consequence to God. This suggests that Job believes that his existence on earth has some, as of yet undefined, purpose and significance to God. Eliphaz will challenge that idea (22:22-23), but seeping through the whole of Job's discourse and the prologue is the idea that God truly delights in the willingly righteous.

Bildad the Shuhite's First Speech (8:1-22)

Bildad was a Shuhite, probably descended from Shuah, Abraham's son by Keturah (Ge 25:1), and along with Eliphaz and Zophar had an Edomite background. The Septuagint records him as a sovereign or ruler of the Shuhites (2:11), possibly the rule of Hadad at the time.

He had neither time for Job's pleas of innocence nor his appeal for a hearing from God. Bildad considered Job to be deserving of his suffering and appealed to ancient tradition as his authority (8:8). He suggested that Job's fortunes might be restored, but gives no condition for that to occur. He finishes with restating the question with which Eliphaz began, "Can a man be righteous before God?" (25:4), indicating some reliance upon Eliphaz.

8:1-7

Bildad suggests that Job is speaking little more than hot air; 'your children got what they deserved'. However, Bildad advises Job to seek God, for if he truly is pure in heart, God will prosper him.

Bildad's impatience with Job is evident from the start of his dialogue as people often are with others who refuse to acknowledge the 'truth' or what is considered to be the 'appropriate course of action'. Bildad begins to build a case for a theologically sound reason for Job's suffering (as a result of his sinfulness) and the remedy. The basis for which Bildad accuses Job's children is unknown and may be pure speculation on his part. It would seem drawn entirely from the result of their demise and his theological conviction that the wicked get punished. In any case, it is hardly an empathetic approach to help a man in great torment and Bildad begins to shed some doubt about Job's righteous state.

Bildad's conclusions regarding Job's present situation are drawn from his clearly-defined theology and it would seem that nothing will dissuade him from that. He seems to ignore Job's past and affirms that if Job is pure and upright, Job will know restoration even though it may start with small beginnings (v. 7). Of course, for Bildad, such an outcome is entirely dependent on Job's purity, which it would seem is in doubt.

As heartless as Bildad appears, it is true that when counselling the counselee needs to be brought to a place where he/she can see reality. However, in Bildad's case, it is he who could not see reality and even if his intentions were good, he was doing Job no good at all. Bildad and Job view the reason for this situation quite differently, therefore, Bildad begins to build a case from tradition to prove his premise to be correct.

8:8-19

Bildad asserts that tradition illustrates that those who neglect God perish; it is after all the self-evident truth of natural law.

The validity of Bildad's assertion that Job will see God if he is indeed pure in heart and seeks Him earnestly is supported by his appeal to the wisdom of traditional understanding using the self-evident truths of nature. He is using a simple cause and effect argument and misapplying it to Job's situation. Therefore, it is not so much what he is saying that is wrong, but the intent of his application. Misapplied truth is usually disastrous and misapplied theological truth is equally disastrous; Jewish first-century national aspirations are a case in point, as such they did not appreciate the Messiah as He walked among them. Perhaps a recent example is the 'prosperity doctrine', which in part says that if a Christian tithes, usually on their gross income, then they will be materially blessed by God. The truth is that God does reward giving (Lk 6:38), but the blessing is not necessarily material. Such promises can lead to impure motives for giving and sometimes equally impure motives for teaching the doctrine. In similar fashion, Bildad's supposition that the righteous are blessed calls into question the motive for righteous living. Job stands astride mixed motives as he holds on to his integrity founded in his disinterested piety.

Bildad applies these self-evident truths to the godless חָנֵף (*hānēp*), which implies the profane; those who forget God[19] (cf. Ps 50:22) or hypocrite.[20] It is unclear if this is a veiled comment on Bildad's suspicion that Job is not nearly as pure in heart as Job suggests or whether he is simply giving an exposition of the consequences of godless living.
As Bildad's last comments in his first speech indicate, at this point at least, there is a willingness to entertain Job's blamelessness.

8:20-22

Bildad suggests that God will restore Job's fortunes and destroy his enemies.

Bildad takes a surprising change of tone at the end of his first speech, which began with a blunt accusation of speaking 'hot air'. He turns from the self-evident truth of the consequences of the godless to a summation of his theology of retribution—the rewards or otherwise for the blameless and the evildoer. He then pronounces a restoration of Job's fortunes,

---

[19] Clines, *Job 1-20*, comment 8:13.
[20] Smick, '*Job*', comment 8:11-19.

however, he gives no condition for this restoration, but states it as a fact. Perhaps such a prediction is said in light of Bildad's confidence that Job will take his 'good' advice and seek after God (v. 5).

Job's Third Speech (9:1-10:22)

9:1-13

Job cannot see how his righteousness can be vindicated by God when it is God who is assailing him and answerable to no one.

Job is willing to admit that Bildad's basic theology is correct, however, he caveats his agreement with, "But how can a mortal be righteous before God?" The sense with which Job is using 'righteous' צָדַק (*sādaq*) is not in the sense that Eliphaz used it (4:17); asking if a man can be perfectly righteous before God, but in the sense of how a man might be publicly vindicated and declared innocent by God. Job contends that God is too powerful, which is evident in His control of the universe, with the freedom to act in ways that are not dependent upon human approval, for him to be able to argue against God.

9:14-20

Job suggests that he would not get a hearing from God and if he did, his state before God would cause him to condemn himself.

Job considers the possibility of bringing God before a court in order for his innocence to be pronounced. This is a vain thought for two reasons, one being it is obvious that Job cannot bring God to court and the second that Job does not believe that God would give him a favourable hearing in any case. As God is the source of his suffering, He would only cause Job to suffer more (v. 17). Job also has a sense of the frailty of his innocence צָדַק (*sādaq*) and blamelessness because even if he were to stand before God his own mouth would condemn him. It is not entirely clear as to why Job would think this, but perhaps in the presence of God, Job a sinner (as in not better than any man), could not possibly plead his right but rather only for mercy from God.

Bildad's advice of looking to God and pleading with Him (8:5) at this point is rejected as worthless along with the hope that Bildad suggested at the end of his speech that Job would see restoration (8:20-21). Job is convinced that God has pronounced him guilty and nothing, not even his innocence, can change that.

9:21-24

Job expresses his observation that it is God who allows the wicked things on earth to happen and his unjust suffering is one of those wicked things.

Job has just contended that if God has chosen to hold Job guilty there is nothing he can do to prove his innocence, however, he insists again (v. 21) his blamelessness and begins to throw caution to the wind by declaring that under the sovereign hand of God all—the righteous and unrighteous—are treated the same. Job is now beginning to break out of the doctrine of retribution as he is willing to admit that it does not always hold true and it is God who allows such chaos, because if not God, then who else allows these things? This issue begins to speak to the heart of the matter in Job—there is evil in the world for which no person has a logical or satisfying explanation.

9:25-31

Job cannot escape his suffering through a change of attitude or a ritual cleansing of himself because he believes that God has found him guilty already.

Job considers two fruitless avenues that he might use to release himself from his suffering; one is to simply ignore his condition and put on a brave face and the other is to purify himself through ritual washing. Job realises that neither of these avenues will grant him what he desires. He cannot simply ignore his immense suffering and if he were to purge himself through ritual washing, such is his belief in God's judgement against him, that God would place him in a worse state, where even his clothes would detest him. Job's days on earth are rushing by and there is nothing he can do, therefore, he thinks that to end this misery is best as God's judgement on him is final.

9:32-35

Job perceives the need for a mediator between

himself and God, but has no hope of one.

Even though Job has argued for his day in court he is aware he cannot confront God in court as an equal. Job wishes for an arbitrator, one who can mediate on his behalf. It is difficult to know if Job means an arbitrator who can settle a dispute and can bring both parties together or an arbiter who is superior to them both, who can impose his authority and thus declare Job innocent. What is clear is that Job has no hope of one. It is too much to infer that Job is predicting the New Testament doctrine of Christ as mediator.[21] Job is not looking for a mediator who can have his sins forgiven, but one who can prove an innocent man innocent. However, there are aspects of a foreshadowing of Christ as mediator, who rather than declaring the innocent as innocent, instead pronounces the guilty innocent through His sacrifice.

10:1-7
Out of Job's distress he finds the courage to complain to God as he believes he has nothing more to lose.

Job is not asking God for healing or restoration of his former life. He can accept that God has the right to act as He chooses (2:10). However, Job's expectation is that God will act in ways that are consistent with justice and, therefore, Job's quest is to have God

---

[21] Smick, 'Job', comment 9:25-35.

explain why He is not acting justly in his case. Job has observed that God allows the wicked at times to prosper (v. 3), therefore, he is also aware that a simplistic understanding of the doctrine of retribution does not contribute to a well-formed worldview. However, he cannot see a reason why God should so severely punish him, in a way in which he is so completely helpless.

10:8-17

After reflecting on the delicate creative concern that God demonstrated over his making, Job asks if God would destroy him, as it now seems to Job that this has been God's intention all along.

Job is suggesting that the lavish kindness that God has previously bestowed upon him was done only to torment him. As Job can see no further future to his life, his end will be in misery made all the worse because he has known the best that life has to offer. It seems to Job that God has intended this all along. Job understands that God's inexorable will is irresistible and he cannot escape, be he guilty or not (vv. 15-16). For whatever reason God has chosen to punish him; the torment is not only relentless, but it intensifies (v. 17).

10:18-22

Job raises the issue of the futility of life, even the futility of God treating him this way and asks if this is God's great purpose for him, concluding that if this is so, then it would be better not to have been born.

Job believes that he has been singled out for special attention, which he has, with no understanding as to why, nor having the remotest glimmer of the truth. Now he ponders why God bothered to have such intricate concern over his birth (vv. 9-12). At this point in time he would have preferred that his life's journey would have been short; from the womb directly to the tomb. This is an idle wish as Job is requesting that God would turn away from him in order that he might have a small amount of joy before his life ends (v. 20). The place of death is just as relentless as Job's life, dark and permanent, and while Job has hoped for death previously there is no sense that this is his first choice, but the choice of a man with no real choice; in death at least, he believes, God will stop tormenting him.

Zophar the Naamathite's First Speech (11:1-20)

Zophar was from Naamah though it is not certain that this Naamah can be associated with the town in Judah in the Shephelah near Lachish (Jos 15:41).[22] He is the harshest of Job's critics, appealing to tradition as did Bildad, but adding 'wisdom'. The Septuagint records him as being a king of the Minaeans (2:11).

Wisdom, according to Job's counselors, entails keeping God's commands and consequently God

---

[22] See Clines, 'Job 1-17", comment 2:11.

rewards God-fearing people with material blessings and health. His argument toward Job centres on demonstrating Job's deceitful and evil ways (11:5-6). Zophar believes that Job can be redeemed by putting away his sin (11:14), but has little hope that Job will as Job has not responded well to Zophar's and the other friend's advice and, therefore, finishes by lecturing Job on the fate of sinners. His contention that Job is a sinner in need of repentance could not be more incorrect and as a result his 'comfort' can only add to Job's suffering.

11:1-6

Zophar asserts that Job is wrong and, therefore, needs to be corrected. He insists that Job is not as righteous as Job thinks he is, to the point where his suffering is light in comparison with
his great sin.

Zophar has listened to both Eliphaz and Bildad and Job's subsequent responses and it is now his time to speak. He begins in the same vein as Bildad (8:2); he is impatient with Job and discredits Job's essential premise that he is a blameless man. Zophar is insistent that Job sees sense of which he, in Zophar's view, is devoid. He asserts that if Job were to stand before God, or at least if God were to speak to Job, Job would find that God would rebuke him and reveal true wisdom—the type that Zophar believes he has and Job has not. Job has claimed to be blameless, but not claimed perfection (7:21). Zophar appreciates none of this, and suggests that at best Job is a secret sinner deserving of his punishment; in fact Zophar implies, that in His mercy, Job is getting off lightly (v. 6).

11:7-9

No one can fathom the mysteries of God and, therefore, Zophar implies that Job is wrong.

Zophar draws attention to the boundless knowledge and presence of God believing that somehow such truth can only serve to affirm Job's helplessness and ignorance (v. 8). This point is made because Zophar asserts that Job is claiming flawless theology (v. 4), and, therefore, superior to theirs. All three friends would agree that clearly Job's theology cannot possibly be the superior because of the evidence of his current desperate situation. This is no argument at all, and while it is true that God's omniscience and omnipresence are immeasurable that does not mean that man cannot know something of God; indeed Zophar is suggesting that he does. The reader knows full well that Zophar has drawn wrong conclusions regarding Job's suffering, and therefore, it is Zophar who is the ignorant one.

11:10-12

No one can contend with God, nor His immutable laws.

Although Zophar is speaking in general terms it is clear that he is pointing his comments at Job. Zophar cannot see beyond his retributionist dogma and, therefore, cannot treat Job as an innocent sufferer and thus is devoid of compassion. Rather, Zophar interprets Job's situation as a guilty man who receives deserved punishment. The point that Zophar is making in v. 12 is that there are some things that will not change; in this context being that the wicked get punished by God. The following verses indicate that Zophar has not lost all hope for Job because although the doctrine of retribution does not change, Job has the capacity to repent and thus find God's blessing again (vv. 15-19).

11:13-20

Zophar counsels that God will accept the penitent and if Job will acknowledge his sin God will bless him again.

Zophar now makes his conclusion about Job explicit—Job is sinful (v. 14). Zophar's advice is that if only Job would רָחַק (*rāhaq*) remove, by driving far from him, the sin that is in his life his fortunes would completely change. However, Zophar implies that if Job would not do what he, so wisely, suggests then Job's end would be miserable with no other hope than to breathe his last breath (v. 20). The repentance that Zophar suggests is good advice to those living in sinful indulgence; however, he has not accepted Job's blameless position. If Eliphaz suggests that Job has sinned slightly and, therefore, Job is soon to be relieved (4:5-6), and Bildad that Job has not sinned so greatly that his life has not been cut off from him, unlike Job's children (8:4-6), Zophar goes a step further suggesting that Job is getting nothing more than deserved punishment; he is suffering greatly because he has been sinning greatly.

All three are convinced of the correctness of their theological position and we can learn the lesson that correlation is not necessarily causation and a superficial reading of a situation can cause a person to draw seriously wrong conclusions. The New Testament affirms this graphically with the image of Jesus hanging on the cross. The Apostle Paul writes that anyone who is hung on a tree is cursed (Gal 3:13); in fact he tells his readers that Jesus became a curse for us. A superficial observation of the scene as many Jews made, would indicate that Jesus was a sinner under God's holy wrath. Only in part is that true; indeed Jesus was under God's wrath, but He was no sinner and the wrath He bore was for humanity's sin collectively, not His own. How dangerous it is for Christians to lock down their thinking into easily definable premises without being prepared to look beyond the scope of their immediate environment. Christian theology celebrates the limitless nature of God, and yet so often Christians are guilty of treating the work of God borne in the lives of His people as being easily definable and limited through their own theology. The story of Job shows us how important it is to seek God for answers and to not rely solely on our limited theology.

Job's Fourth Speech (12:1-14:22)

12:1-3

Using pointed sarcasm, Job maintains that his friends' wisdom is not superior to his as they have only voiced common knowledge.

Job has now heard all three of his friends speak and not one of them has appreciated his unique situation. Job believes in the doctrine of retribution along with his friends, but for him something is seriously wrong because he knows, according to the doctrine, he does not deserve suffering, rather the opposite. Job's friends, however, cannot conceive of Job's innocence because the evidence of his great suffering is proof positive of his sinfulness, secret or otherwise. Therefore, Job's friends only speak from conventional wisdom, which Job supports in general although he knows that conventional wisdom does not supply a satisfactory answer to his question of his suffering.

12:4-6

In his state of undeserved suffering, Job has lost the respect he once held and laments that the unrighteous suffer no such chastisement.

Job was more than a moral, respected, wealthy landowner; he also had a priestly function, and it would seem more than just to his own family (1:5). In v. 4 he recounts that he was a man intimate with God to the point where God would answer his prayer. In any religious culture, ancient or modern, respect naturally follows such an obvious connection with the divine. However, now that God is not answering Job and seemingly cursing him, the respect he once held has vanished. Human beings tend to be fickle and follow and admire the successful, but once that success has vanished, so too the adoring crowds. Job feels this sharply because of his innocence. He in himself knows that nothing has changed within, yet he must suffer insult in addition to his injury as this is a principle by which the culture around Job lives; the suffering deserve further rebuke.[23] Not only does Job bemoan the fact that the שָׁדַד (*šādad*), marauders [NIV], who are more than robbers [NRSV, AMP, KJV], but brigands—professional plunderers, like pirates, or perhaps like the Sabeans and Chaldeans (1:15,17) who carried off his flocks and herds—are also people in God's hands, and though idolatrous and carry on their dishonest lifestyle seem to receive no visible rebuke from God.

12:7-12

Natural law demonstrates that God controls all things, but for Job that does not mean that all goes well with the innocent.

Tribulation has a way of causing people to re-evaluate their beliefs. Job has ascribed to the doctrine of retribution, but the theology does not now fit with

---

[23] Clines, *Job 1-20*, comment 12:4-6.

his personal experience and perhaps forces him to reconsider issues that he has not up to this point considered much before. While affirming the absolute sovereignty of God, to which all the characters in this drama agree, Job focuses on the negative aspects (from a human perspective) of God's sovereign activity. He asserts that even the dumb of God's creation, the animals, birds and fish, understand how God works. Simply observing the brutality in nature affirms for Job that not all that God does is moral and good, from a human perspective, as his friends seem to affirm. Job insists by referring to the ear testing words (v. 11) and wisdom coming to those who have lived a long time (v. 12), that his assertions about God's justice, or lack of it, is obvious.

12:13-25

God is sovereign over all life, and while His hand can be obviously seen, a person does not necessarily understand God's purposes.

Here Job conveys his wisdom compared with that of his friends; he understands the true nature of God's power and activity, which is deeper than his friends can comprehend. Eliphaz earlier expounded on how everything good comes to the righteous (5:18-26). Here, in direct contrast, Job declares how God's power operates in the social sphere in ways which are often subversive or destructive. These are things that he has observed (13:1), and, of course, painfully knows from his own experience. Therefore, he affirms that he is just as wise as his friends and, moreover, the wisdom of God is beyond his friends as they cannot seem to appreciate that bad things happen to good people. Job wants to address God because he doesn't understand his situation; his friends perceive this as a lack of wisdom because their understanding is neatly packaged.

13:1-12

Job acknowledges that he has observed the sovereign hand of God at work in the world and is insulted by his friends' platitudes and comments about him which he knows are wrong.

Job is insulted by his friends' accusations of guilt and calls their wisdom into question. He gains no comfort from them, only poor advice based on their misunderstanding of Job's situation. Such was the lack of help his friends' wisdom has given him, Job very curtly suggests that silence is a better option for them; this is in the same vein as Proverbs 17:28. Though these are men of wisdom Job is not so subtly calling them fools. Therefore, with no earthly help, Job has no other recourse except to appeal to God.

13:13-19

With no help coming from his friends, Job declares his certainty that he will be vindicated if he can defend himself before God.

Job declares his boldness to present his case before

God and in so doing he is using this as evidence before his friends as proof of his innocence, which they struggle to accept. There is much scholarly debate as to whether Job has hope in God or not (v. 15). David Clines' alternative translation: "He may slay me; I am without hope. Yet I will defend my conduct to his face."[24] Is more in line with the NRSV than KJV, NASB, NIV, which suggest Job has an inherent trust in God. It appears that the Hebrew can be read both ways. However, the main issue that Job has is not with his faith in God, God's faith in him, or from Job's perspective, God's seeming lack of it. His confidence lies in his innocence, knowing that no one can charge him with evil (v. 19) although Eliphaz attempts to do so (22:5-11) without success. Job will continue to declare his innocence and walk uprightly before God no matter what happens.

13:20-28

Job requests, again, an audience with God believing his innocence will vindicate him and God will see the pointlessness of harassing Job in the way He has done.

Job is using the language of the law court in his appeal to God. He places two conditions on God which are necessary for Job to speak; one, to withdraw His hand (of torment) and two, to stop frightening Job with terrors. These conditions are very much linked to

---

[24] Clines, *Job 1-20*, comment 13:15.

Job's initial response of not cursing God. Perhaps Job fears that if God were to lay an even heavier burden upon him then he wouldn't have the courage to speak before God. Upon making the request, Job then continues to question the sense of God tormenting him in the way He has. Job realises that it is pointless to count a person as an enemy when he is devoted and, therefore, Job continues to soul search for the reason; perhaps it is because of the sins of his youth (v. 26).

14:1-6

Job acknowledges the limits to life that God has decreed, but requests that God would leave him alone until he has done his time.

Job regresses from his spirited request for an audience with God into a state of general hopelessness for the human race. Pressing upon Job's perspective is his current situation which has become the lens through which he now views life. So much of human perspective is context specific and in Job's case the good of the past is dwarfed in the tsunami of the present. It is interesting to note that more often than not the bad of a person's past has a far stronger impact on the present than the good of the past. Therefore, while speaking of the human race in general, more specifically he is thinking of himself, knowing his days are allotted and from which there is no escape whether in life or death, thus likening his existence to that of a hired man. Job also used this analogy of the hired man in 7:1; he has to do his inescapable time, therefore,

'Please God, leave me alone,' is his request.

14:7-12

Job contrasts his hopelessness with that of a tree which can spring back to life, whereas he cannot.

The stump of evidence of what Job once was still remains. In comparison, Job states that the stump of a felled tree has more hope than man because the stump can sprout new life. Not so for man; once he breathes his last he is no more and has no hope of resurrection in this life as the tree might. Not until the heavens have vanished is there any possibility of hope, as Job is about to mention (v. 14).

14:13-17

Job wishes God to end his suffering in death and then raise him up after His anger has passed as Job is certain that then his good relationship with God will be restored.

Job suggests that there is hope for him beyond the grave. Job reasons that if God would hide him in Sheol (that is take his life) until the cause of God's anger with him has passed, then at his renewal, his benevolent God will long for him and whatever sin Job has committed God will cover. To the extent that this is a strong theological idea or a whimsical hope on Job's part we cannot be sure, however, it is certainly a foreshadowing of the Christian hope of resurrection.

14:18-22

Job asserts that God takes hope of life away and human suffering is all-consuming, even beyond the grave.

Job rebounds into hopelessness again as he compares the unalterable effects of erosion on rock with God destroying hope beyond the grave. There is no shortage of objects to the testament of this human hope, but no matter how strong and secure such a hope might be, Job asserts that God destroys it. Once dead, people know nothing of this world, according to Job, nor are they concerned, for their only concern is with their own suffering. This is one of the rare places in the Old Testament where feelings are attributed to the dead; not until Jesus tells the story of Lazarus and the Rich Man (Lk 16:19-31) do such ideas appear again. Like the Rich Man, Job sees that the dead languish in self-pity.

Eliphaz's Second Speech (15:1-35)

15:1-6

Eliphaz contends, like Bildad, that Job utters words that are more than useless and adds that they would also lead people astray, which confirms his sin.

Eliphaz's frustration with Job is heightened. Job has not accepted his (wise) words, neither Bildad's nor Zophar's, instead, Job has continued to defend himself and cry out to God for a hearing in order to receive vindication. To Eliphaz, Job's talk is nonsense and if taken seriously, he believes, would lead others into impiety. As Eliphaz hears the expression out of the abundance of Job's heart (cf. Mt 12:34) it confirms to him that Job is a sinful man.

15:7-16

Eliphaz seeks to gain credibility in order for Job to follow his advice, and in so doing he feels he must undermine Job and defend God against him.

Eliphaz's concern for Job is sincere, if not sincerely wrong, and he seeks to establish his credibility—the voice of reason—in order that Job would heed his advice which will result in the restoration of his fortunes. To establish his credibility, in part, Eliphaz discredits Job. However, the reader knows from the prologue and God's response at the end of the drama, in an ironic twist, that the opposite is the case. Adding to the irony is v. 8 where Eliphaz rhetorically asks Job if he has listened in on God's council. Eliphaz probably is thinking in terms of creation, rather than on Job's situation, but it is, of course, the drama in the heavenly council that has brought this crisis about. Job is crying out for an audience with God precisely because he does not understand what is happening to him; if he did understand we would have a very different story. Similarly, if Eliphaz had listened in on the events between God and Satan, he too would take a completely different approach. Instead, locked into his doctrine of retribution, he cannot see anything but Job's obvious sinfulness, despite Job's protestations otherwise. Eliphaz is frustrated because Job will not heed his good advice.

Eliphaz attempts to establish his credibility before Job and he uses a similar approach to Job. He appeals to the collective wisdom of the aged, on which they both agree (12:12). He also places himself on at least the same level of understanding (intelligence) as Job (vv. 8-9), as Job has also appealed for himself (12:3). To the outside observer it becomes clear that this is a debate that neither can win. A significant difference between the two men is that Eliphaz sees himself clearly sided with God; even God's spokesperson (v. 11) as he has spoken gently with Job. Job, however, considers himself abandoned by God; he cannot speak for God, nor understand His ways anymore. Job, according to Eliphaz, has no right to take his mercurial stance against God (v. 13) because he, like any man, is not pure enough to do so.

15:17-26

The collective wisdom of the age declares that it is the wicked who are punished and knowing their evil deeds, they live in fear of death.

Eliphaz recounts his observations of how the wicked suffer because of their rebellion toward God (v. 25). For Eliphaz this is proof positive of the doctrine of retribution at work. Job uses a similar phrase, "My eyes have seen all this..." (13:2). Job's focus though, is not on the wicked being punished, rather God's sovereign hand over all the affairs of humanity and how it is not simply the wicked who suffer and not the righteous that prosper. Despite the fact that Eliphaz's confirmation of his truth comes from the collective wisdom handed down, as Job points out, it is not always the case that the wicked suffer as he describes. Perhaps Eliphaz is so concerned with winning his argument and bringing Job to repentance that he is blinded to the greater truth around him.

15:27-35

Before death comes the wicked will be punished for their evil deeds (v. 32), of which, Eliphaz implies, Job is in danger.

It would be difficult to see Eliphaz applying the behaviour of the wicked and their due punishment explicitly to Job, but rather presenting a general description of the fate of the inherently wicked. Job is not such a man, as Eliphaz knows, but his fear is that Job is moving down a path leading to wickedness. Clearly, to Eliphaz, Job has sinned. How greatly he thinks Job has sinned we cannot know, but he believes Job is certainly increasing his sinfulness (vv. 4-6, 13). By pointing to the fate of the wicked, Eliphaz wishes to wake Job to the fact that he is walking down a dangerous path. At the end of his first speech Eliphaz looked forward to a time of restoration of Job's fortunes (5:20-26) because his suffering was the necessary correcting hand of God upon Job's life (5:17), if Job would follow Eliphaz's advice (5:27). Job, however, did not accept his advice, nor the advice of his other friends, therefore, at the end of his second speech, Eliphaz is subtly alluding to Job's fate if he will not listen to him.

Job's Fifth Speech (16:1-17:16)

16:1-5

Job contends that if his friends were in a similar situation he would bring them comfort. They, however, are no comfort at all.

The issue of expectations becomes very pointed with Job's opening response to Eliphaz. It seems reasonable to suggest that, along with Job, his friends want Job's suffering to end. Job believes that the only way it can end is if he can make his appeal directly to God who, he is certain, will vindicate him. His friends however, believe that only when Job turns away from his sin will his fortunes change. This is when expectations clash; because Job believes that there can be no reversal until he can speak with God, nothing that counsellors can do or say will change anything. Therefore, Job is looking for friends who will commiserate with him. His friends however, expect Job to heed their wise words, which will, they believe, bring the reversal that they all want. As a result they have different expectations regarding their roles; empathy or advice. They do not want to comfort Job and Job does not want their advice, hence he calls them miserable comforters (v. 2).

Job suggests that if they were in his situation he would comfort and encourage them (v. 5). This may well be the case, however, to be fair to his friends, if they had an accurate understanding of the situation, they may well have indeed been of more comfort and encouragement. But, of course, they don't and refuse to accept Job's protestations regarding his innocence. Therefore, no matter how sincere, they cannot be of any help to Job.

Job's comments here are very pertinent to those who, for whatever reason, seek to counsel. The question that should be foremost in the counsellor's mind is not the rights or wrongs of the situation. For the most part people presenting for counselling consider themselves to be the aggrieved in some way, as does Job. In Job's situation he is correct, however, that truth cannot always be assumed, therefore, the counsellor firstly needs to ascertain what it is that the counselee wants; comfort or advice. Unwanted advice serves no good purpose and often ends up aggrieving both parties, similarly, unwanted comfort is equally ineffectual.

16:6-14

Job speaks to God of the unending anguish that He has placed upon him, pointing out that God has used men to inflict much of this suffering.

From Job's perspective it is not just God who

attacks him, but also men. We cannot be sure if Job has been physically harmed in his weakened state (v. 10) or whether this is a hyperbole as in his descriptions of God's attacks upon him (vv. 13-14). If Job's friends are representative of the culture of the day, then the people around him would have drawn the same conclusions; that Job was suffering due to his sinfulness. That being the case, they could well have been abusive toward him. Job has already described himself as a laughing stock to his friends (12:4) and later further elaborates on his suffering from men (19:13-19; 30:9-10). As has already been noted in comment 12:4-6, it is not uncommon to add insult to injury. Job certainly could be justified in describing himself as being handed over to evil men (v. 11) as it was arguably wicked men (the Sabeans and Chaldeans) who took all his livestock through which much of his prosperity was earned. All this suffering though, very clearly in Job's mind, is the hand of God (v. 11) against him.

16:15-17

Job continues to plead his righteousness.

Such is the depth of Job's anguish and the permanence with which he believes it will reside with him, he speaks of sewing sackcloth, the traditional material for mourning, onto his very skin. Grief has become permanent and inseparable from him. These are, in one sense, symbols of Job's innocence; there is little place to mourn for just treatment. Therefore, in symbol and word, Job continues to protest his innocence.

16:18-21

Job speaks of an advocate in heaven who will plead his case for him.

If death before his acquittal is his likely destiny, then Job wants a memorial to his innocence. Blood, unless covered, cries out to heaven in vengeance just as Abel's blood cried out (Ge 4:10-11) against his brother. Job, too, wants his blood to bear witness to the great wrong done to him and from Job's perspective, both God and the wicked are on the same side opposing him (v. 11). Yet, despite this final appeal Job begins to speak of an advocate, which he made reference to in 16:19. Here he seems more certain of the existence of his advocate. Job does not expand on the idea except that the advocate will plead with God on behalf of man. In the next part of his monologue, Job sees nothing for himself but the grave. However, later Job further expands on his eschatological hope (19:25-27), though how well formed it is, is unclear. The language used, however, fits perfectly with the role of Christ Jesus (1Ti 2:5); that, in my opinion, is a prophetic Christological prefiguring, which is, in light of redemptive history, a better interpretation than Job's blood being his advocate.[25]

---

[25] See Clines, *Job*, comment 16:1-17:16.

16:22-17:5

With a sense of desperation stemming from his perceived soon-to-be demise, Job pleads for God's vindication because men are blinded to his innocence.

Job reverts to his sense of hopelessness where only Sheol awaits while only hostile mocking people surround him. Job asks God for a pledge and Elmer Smick's paraphrase is helpful for understanding 'the pledge you demand' (v. 3); "Give attention (O God) to becoming my guarantor (that I am right) with you, for who else will shake my hand to prove it?"[26] Without God's vindication, Job is assured of no human sympathy at all.

Men and women suffering as a result of others being blinded to innocence is a strong biblical theme; Jesus, Joseph, Daniel, David and Mary to name a few. It is a frightening situation especially when it is the people of God who are blinded. Spiritual blindness is expected for those who will not believe, but what is the root of the spiritual blindness of those who claim faith? Often it is because their values and their core allegiance are found in one of three, or a combination of these three areas; one, there is allegiance to the flesh (self); two, continual acceptance of the values of the collective wisdom of the age; and three, the collective wisdom of their religious practice. Without the transformation of the 'new birth' (1Pe 1:3ff.; 1Jn 3:9) those who claim to believe are blinded and cannot see

---

[26] Smick, *Job*, comment 17:3-5.

God, nor sense His Spirit (see Jn 5:37-40) because there is no real allegiance to the kingdom of God. Unless Christians are rooted in the kingdom of God with its commensurate relationship with God and abiding in the kingdom's values, there can be no motivating love (*agapē*) and any love that is demonstrated is self-driven.

Without Christians not only belonging to the kingdom of God through faith in Christ Jesus, but also living the values of the kingdom of God, it is too easy to be blinded to what God is doing in and through others and subsequently treat the innocent as guilty. This is the situation for Job because there is no appreciation of God's activities beyond, at best, a rudimentary understanding. Since God makes it clear in Isaiah that His ways are higher than that of humans (Isa 55:8-9) then it is imperative that the Christian, when making decisions for or determining attitudes about others, don't simply work with assumptions as Job's friends did. The Spirit of God has been given to God's people and the imperative is to seek God, asking Him to reveal His purposes in and through others in order that wrong conclusions are avoided. Had this been Job's friends' response to the discrepancy between their theological understanding and Job's protestations that they were wrong, and he was in fact innocent, then they could well have been encouraging comforters. Instead, they not only misrepresented Job, but also God (42:7-8).

17:6-9

Job suffers even at the hands of the morally upright because they consider him to be an ungodly person.

Job is certain that his reputation, now as a great sinner, travels before him and people spit in his face as a strong expression of contempt. The grief that Job feels at the overwhelming injustice has affected him physically (v. 7). The injustice against him has also come from the upright, who naturally strengthen their position by condemning the ungodly; the great irony being that Job is not to be counted among the ungodly. As people satisfy their strong sense of moral indignation toward Job, they show themselves to be weak in insight.

17:10-16

As nobody has the wisdom to understand Job's predicament and thus they treat him cruelly, he finds that he has no other hope than death in order to escape his misery.

Job's contention that he will not find wisdom (among you [v. 10]) is most likely to be directed to the righteous in general, as it appears all have assumed his guilt, and so he slips again into depression as he recounts the loss of his hope (desires of his heart). Zophar has already declared that Job's darkness will be turned to light (if Job heeds his words [11:17]), however, Job regards them as men who cannot tell when darkness is near and instead call it light (v. 12).

Therefore, Job returns to his idea that he has no other hope than the grave (Sheol). It is not that he wants that, but he can see no other possible escape from his misery.

Bildad's Second Speech (18:1-21)

18:1-4

Bildad has taken offense at Job's assertion that he, Eliphaz and Zophar do not know what they are talking about—it is Bildad's contention that it is Job who needs to come to his senses.

Bildad is affronted by Job's claim of innocence in the face of such obvious guilt, recognisable by his suffering. Not only that, he is offended by Job's assertion that they are ignorant, when from Bildad's perspective, Job is irrationally self-centred. Bildad's perspective is that the universe is set and Job is calling for the unchangeable to change, which, for Bildad, it cannot, therefore, Job needs to come to his senses.

18:5-21

Bildad reiterates his theology regarding the fate of the wicked. The inference being that Job is in danger of this fate.

From Bildad's perspective Job does not fully understand the doctrine of retribution as Job tediously bemoans how the righteous suffer and the wicked prosper. He not only wants to set the record straight for Job, but not too deeply veiled in his exposition is the accusation that, "You, Job, are such a man." His illustration of the fate of the wicked—lack of offspring (v. 19)—must have been very pointed to Job as his children were all taken from him. Job has told of how appalled the righteous have been concerning him (17:8) and it would seem that Bildad has come to the point of suggesting that Job does not know God (v. 21). Bildad, from the beginning, had no time for Job's words (8:1) and now that it seems that Job will in no way accept his (good) advice, which demands that Job turn back to God, therefore, naturally in Bildad's mind Job must be consigned as one of the wicked.

Job's Sixth Speech (19:1-29)

19:1-6

Job is crushed by Bildad's (and the others') words and insists that if he has gone astray it is none of their business, however, Job has not, and asserts again that he has not sinned but has been wronged by God.

To be fair to Bildad (and the others), he meant Job no harm, in fact the opposite. However, because Bildad could not appreciate Job's predicament as a result of his theology, which reduced God and his actions to an easily discernible formula, he is unable to show any mercy toward Job. Job finds Bildad's words to be devastating and the 'ten times' (v. 3) he has been reproached ought to be understood in the sense of being rebuked in full measure. Then Job makes the point that if he has sinned, not that he is admitting to it, then that is purely between him and God. This statement is made because of his friends' intransigence as to accepting his innocence. But the idea that personal sin is of no one else's concern is not strictly correct. Rarely do our sins against God (Ps 51:4) have no impact on those around us. Jesus tells his disciples to speak to the person who has sinned and bring in the elders if he will not respond (Mt 18:15-17). Paul (Gal 6:1) and James (5:19) issue similar commands. Here Job has, perhaps, gone too far in saying that if he had sinned it was his concern alone (v. 4). The point that Job is making is that his friends, instead of helping, are destroying him by standing in judgement over him because they cannot accept, as Job states again (v. 6), that it is God who has wronged him.

19:7-12

Job knows that he is powerless to change his situation because it is God who has overwhelmed him.

Job declares not only his sense of abandonment by God, especially in terms of his defence, but also that God is at war with him; the protector has now become the attacker. The analogy that Job gives is that God is attacking him as an army attacks a fortified city, which from Job's perspective is complete overkill because he is no fortified city, just a vulnerable tent (v. 12). Job has no one to turn to and, therefore, no justice (v. 7).

19:13-20

Job laments how God has caused him to be humiliated in the eyes of all men including those closest to him—so weakened he cannot defend himself and barely survives (v. 20).

Not only does Job feel that he has been abandoned by God, but he also believes that God has caused people to abandon him as well. Job's skin disease, which would have been feared as contagious, meant he would have been avoided; that, along with his obvious suffering, perceived as being caused by his sinfulness, meant that Job truly had nothing—no family, no home, no embrace of human kindness, and possibly no intimacy with his wife (v. 17). In this lament we see that Satan has left Job with absolutely nothing except his life. What does Job have? Even his bones cling to his skin;[27] such is Job's complaint that he says that even his bones have lost their vigour and hang upon the flesh (v. 20). Thus this proverbial saying means that the margin between life and death for him is so infinitesimal that it cannot be seen; Job considers himself, for all intents and purpose, the living dead.

19:21-22

Job asks for pity from his friends implying that their treatment of him is no less devastating than

---

[27] The NRSV translates this verse better than the NIV which does not translate דָּבֵק(dabaq); cling or cleave.

God's.

After describing his extreme case of suffering, Job pleads for pity. His description is no exaggeration; even his friends were appalled at his great suffering when they first saw him (2:13). However, now that they have drawn their conclusions regarding his suffering they will not show pity for him. Job asks why they treat him in the same way that he perceives God does. The reader could well ask why his friends would treat him in the same way that Satan does. However, the reader has understanding of the heavenly drama of which Job and his friends are unaware. For the reader this stands as a stark reminder that even in seeking to defend God, as Job's friends are seeking to do, they are in fact aiding Satan's cause. Many times within church history men have sought to uphold what they believed to be the right of God, but in so doing destroyed Jesus' new command (Jn 13:34-35),[28] and unwittingly become the agents of Satan.

19:23-27

Job desires for his words to be a permanent record of his innocence for a time will come when he will see his Redeemer and be acquitted.

---

[28] The reformers Luther and Zwingli's attitude toward the Anabaptists is a case in point. Accused of sedition, these Christians, who believed that the Sermon on the Mount must be obeyed, were put to death in their thousands.

Job would have his words permanently recorded so that one day he would be vindicated, contending against Bildad who has suggested that Job would be completely forgotten (18:17; cf. Pr 10:7). Job is now suggesting that his vindication will not come within the timeframe of his remaining life, however he is well aware that his vindication can come from only one source; his redeemer can be none other than God himself. Some commentators disagree, suggesting that as Job believes that it is God who is afflicting him it is, therefore, exceedingly unlikely that Job would then consider God to be his Redeemer or the means to his redemption and vindication, making God appear as vindicator and legal attorney against himself.[29] Such thinking seems to miss the point, when in Job's mind it can only be God who can vindicate him. Certainly Job sees God acting as his enemy (13:24), but he also believes that if he can argue his case before God then he will be vindicated (13:18). Job is dealing with the perplexity of God's dealing with him, and while he may consider God to be acting as his enemy there is no sense that Job is God's enemy. The sense the reader is given is that Job believes that if he can speak with God this awful situation will be put right (13:8; cf. 23:4-7). At the present point in the dialogue Job cannot see his vindication within his lifetime, however, he still has hope that he will, indeed, be vindicated by God. God then is his Redeemer גֹּאֵל (*go'al*), and Job has a hope, perhaps only a vague hope, that he will see God

---

[29]See Clines discussion on this, Clines, *Job 1-20*, comment 19:25-27.

beyond the grave and the thought warms the righteous man.

19:28-29

Job turns the tables on his friends by suggesting that their treatment of him will result in their judgement.

Job addresses his friends again, with a sense of new-found confidence, and paraphrasing vv. 28-29 that, "If you think I am the author of my own misfortune (because of my sin) then you should be very careful; you are wrong and judgement will fall on you." Such a statement will not endear Job's friends toward him, but it is the truth.

Zophar's Second Speech (20:1-29)

20:1-3

Zophar, like Bildad, is compelled to justify himself in the face of Job's rebuke, rather than bring comfort.

In Job's last statement (19:28-29) he has turned his friends' warnings against him onto them, stating that they are the ones in danger of punishment. Job has attacked Zophar's worldview, and it is upon his worldview that Zophar relies for security. If Job was correct, that would mean according to Zophar's worldview that Zophar is the one guilty of sin, which of course, he is certain that he is not. Therefore, he will appeal to ancient tradition in order to prove his credibility with Job.

20:4-11

Zophar expounds his theology of the wicked being punished for their wrongdoing and as with Bildad, the inference is that Job is suffering because of his wickedness—proof of his understanding (v. 3) is found in Job's circumstances in a simple cause and effect paradigm.

Zophar's credibility lies squarely with ancient tradition (v. 4), as does Bildad's (8:8ff), and he has nothing new to say to Job. Instead, he speaks more passionately (louder) about the fate of the wicked. When frustrated, people often resort to shouting the same words they have previously used when initially misunderstood; as if volume brings clarification. Job had made a case for the wicked prospering (10:3 cf. 21:7-13) of which Zophar will have no part. It would appear that he is blinded to the times when the wicked do prosper (v. 5) and certainly where their joy lasts longer than a moment. It is not as if all that Zophar is saying is wrong in relation to the fate of the wicked in this life, but the categorical nature in which he applies the truth makes him sound absurd. [30] Secondly, his application of this truth upon Job is completely misplaced. However, from Zophar's perspective, all the justification that he has heard from Job simply confirms his assertion of Job's sin (11:14), from which Job will not turn.

20:12-29

Zophar expounds the fate of the wicked, levelling a veiled accusation that he places Job among the wicked.

Zophar is explicit about the type of sin of which he is thinking (v. 19); the ill treatment of the poor, which

---

[30] Even Jeremiah asks the question of God about the prospering of the wicked (12:1). The Psalmists answer this perplexing issue to some extent (Psalms 37, 73), wherein ultimately the fate of the wicked is destruction. Why should God allow the wicked to prosper in this life? Obviously not all the wicked prosper and their fate in this life is very much as Job's three friends portray, but not all. Likewise, as in Job's case, for a time at least, not all the righteous prosper in this life. Human beings as a whole want to prosper, and many people are frustrated by relative poverty brought about by honest labour, when it appears the unscrupulous are prospering. The temptation for the righteous is to give up and pursue a less ethical means of living, justifying their behaviour because righteousness has not paid off. Perhaps this is the crux of the issue; the choice that temptation offers in the face of unjust reward. Will a righteous man remain righteous when a better standard of living is afforded by unrighteous actions? Another question to which this naturally leads is, which God are we serving? Job, in the face of the severest of temptation to give up integrity and turn against God, refuses to do so even when God's dealing with him is inexplicable.

leads to quick punishment. This veiled accusation against Job is made explicit by Eliphaz's next speech (22:5-11) and later denied by Job (29:12-17). The caveat given to Job is that these serious consequences will befall him if he does not follow Zophar's advice (11:13-14); similarly Bildad's (8:5). In Zophar's theology, there is no room for repentance or compassion for Job. His concern is with the material whereas Job is more concerned with his relationship with God (19:23-27). Zophar does not speak again.

Job's Seventh Speech (21:1-34)

21:1-3

Job requests that his friends listen to him again although he holds out little hope that they will agree with his argument.

Though Job thinks it is futile he asks his friends to listen to him again. He has given up hope that they will appreciate his situation or his perspective that the wicked do not always suffer. Perhaps, as Zophar has just restated his position with more force in the hope that Job would come to his senses, Job does the same. Although Job restates his position, and would like his friends to agree, he knows that would be unlikely. They have not specifically mocked him, but have accused him of being deserving of this punishment, which is a mockery to Job because he knows he is innocent.

21:4-16

Job wants answers from God—illustrating how God allows those who blaspheme and reject Him to flourish.

Job asks two questions; the first to show that his complaint is not with people or with his friends in particular, and the second, to show that his complaint is turned toward God alone. Such is the misery he faces both physically and psychologically, his whole worldview has fallen apart and he believes it to be more than reasonable to get an answer from the God he has feared and worshiped throughout his life about why this has happened to him. However, such questioning of God is far too impious for his friends.

Job was aware that the wicked, at times, prospered before his suffering, but now in his miserable state, this issue takes on bigger proportions. When life was good the issue may not have been quite so vexing, after all he was arguably far more prosperous than they. Now, in his humbled state the prosperity of the wicked is nothing but scandalous and shakes him to his very core. Everything about Job's life has been at the extremes; it was once (and will be again) extremely good, his relationship with God was extremely close and his devotion extremely pious. At this point he is suffering in the extreme and feels an extreme case of injustice and it is regarding this injustice that God allows, that he wishes to vocalise. The wicked prosper and not only that, they blaspheme and actively reject God (vv. 14-15). Job has no intention of joining with them, he knows that their prosperity also comes from God, but he will not join with them; prosperity in life is not the core issue with Job.

Like all prosperous people, the prosperous wicked Job describes are ready to counsel. Not only that, less prosperous people yearn for such counsel in the hopes that they might profit from it. Job, however, has no interest in such counsel because it comes from an unbelieving heart, that cannot acknowledge or appreciate that their prosperity is not simply a result of their own labours—that the concept of the 'self-made man' is a myth. They have nothing to offer Job; his attitude is echoed by the Psalmist (Ps 37:1-9).

21:17-21

Rather than prospering, Job believes that the wicked should face judgement themselves, not have it delayed for others to receive.

Job takes issue with conventional wisdom in relation to the idea that punishment for the wicked is stored up for the next generation (v. 19 ...*it is said*). Such judgement, he believes, is pointless because the wicked man does not suffer. The reader can almost hear Job saying, "If I have to suffer in my righteousness, then they should be suffering for their wickedness, but they are not." The good the wicked receive is from God, the punishment also is from God, as was both Job's prosperity and suffering. There is no suggestion that God is not in control of this, but the what and why of it, only God knows. To Job it makes no sense that in an ordered universe the wicked are not punished because then that also means there is no reason for the righteous to be rewarded. Wisdom seeks to give the answers to the big questions about life and all the participants in the dialogue are considered to be wise men, but Job is the only one who can see a discrepancy between the doctrine of retribution and experience.

21:22-26

Job concedes that it makes no difference if a man is good or bad, the end is just the same for both.

"Can anyone teach knowledge to God...?" (v. 22) means who can tell God what to do since He judges all; God will do what God will do. The wicked and the righteous end up in the dust and God makes no distinction between the two. This is not simply a contrast and comparison between the wicked and the righteous, but rather there is no simple cause and effect for the benefits received in life or not, but whether good or bad, the end is just the same. God's sovereign and inexplicable hand is over it all and nothing can change what man might think ought to be changed. Job is not trying to change anything, but believes he has a right to an answer; later he will discover he has no right and will humbly relinquish his request (42:1ff.).

21:27-33

Job is well aware of the argument that his friends

are making against him, but if he can get them to concede that there are certainly times when the wicked prosper, then surely there are times when the opposite could also be true.

Job knows that his friends' argument rests upon their observation of his circumstances and, therefore, they conclude that he must be deserving of punishment. But by drawing their attention to the observable fact that there are times when the wicked do indeed prosper, both in life and death, then surely the opposite must be true also—that the righteous do indeed suffer as he has been saying all along. If Job can get them to concede the observable prospering of the wicked then they might be able to concede to his situation and stop wronging him (v. 27). Here he suggests that surely they have canvassed more than their immediate locale, but also spoken to travellers. If so, then surely such people will have confirmed to them what Job has been saying about the lack of punishment for the wicked.

21:34

Experience testifies to the truth of Job's arguments and, therefore, his friends' counter-arguments are false.

Job began by asking his friends to listen to him again, and in returning to that idea at the end of this speech, he rather sharply condemns their arguments as falsehoods because, clearly, their doctrine of retribution is not absolute truth. This is observable in life, and not the truth in Job's life.

Eliphaz's Third Speech (22:1-30)

22:1-3

Eliphaz contends that God is not in need of man and a man's righteousness is of no benefit to Him.

Eliphaz has understood the point of Job's previous speech; that if the wicked prosper then the righteous can suffer, but he is having none of it. As he begins his speech we are given further insight into Eliphaz's theology of an impersonal God. He asserts that God stands to gain nothing from human behaviour as God is not affected in any way. If God brings suffering upon a person, it is not to God that we look for an explanation, as if He has something to gain or lose. The only place for an explanation for human suffering is the person themselves. Job has already stated that his friends will say that the root of the matter lies with him; that is, Job (19:28) and since God is not immoral, according to Eliphaz, Job must be suffering for his wickedness. However, the reader knows that God is extremely concerned with human behaviour and, in this case, particularly Job's. It was God who pointed out the man to Satan (1:8; 2:3) and it is God who has placed this test of disinterested piety upon Job, which will prove Satan's accusations wrong (1:9-11; 2:4-5).

22:4-11

Eliphaz now bluntly states that Job's great suffering has come upon him because of his great sin.

Eliphaz has no place for the idea that God is rebuking Job for his piety; Job, of course, has not suggested that possibility. Job has no idea why God is punishing him, but as Job asserts, and the reader knows from the prologue, it is not as a result of his sin. Eliphaz is, therefore, suggesting possible sins, rather than actual ones. If these accusations against Job were true, the reader would have to re-evaluate the whole book of Job. However, there are no obvious sins that can be levelled against Job, so Eliphaz is inventing social sin which, in his mind, must be great because Job's suffering is great. Eliphaz becomes pointed and blunt; frustrated at Job's unwillingness to heed the rebuke of his friends, which would restore him, he therefore, declares that it is these sins, of which there is no evidence, for which he suffers so terribly (vv. 10-11).

22:12-20

Eliphaz maintains that Job is wrong regarding the extent of God's knowledge—he contends that God sees all—Job, though, has not argued for a limited God.

Eliphaz contends that God is high enough above to see all that goes on in the earth and accuses Job of saying, "What does God know?" Job has not made such an accusation. In Ch. 21 Job recounts how the wicked prosper; that is not a case of God not knowing, but the opposite, and approving. However, Eliphaz will not engage with Job's argument and continues to question Job over his evil ways (v. 15). Eliphaz points out again the fate of the wicked, even when the wicked reject God (v. 16). Eliphaz counts himself as one of the righteous who rejoice over the destruction of the wicked. He quotes the same sentiment as Job (v. 18; 21:16) for similar reasons, but Eliphaz is now convinced that Job is counted amongst the wicked and perhaps this is why Eliphaz has no more to say after the end of this speech.

22:21-30

Eliphaz's final counsel to Job is to repent in order for restoration to come to him.

In the same manner as Bildad (cf. 8:5 ff.), Eliphaz exhorts Job to return to God (v. 23), repent and pray to God, and God will restore him. This is very good advice for a wayward person, but as Eliphaz's diagnosis is wrong so too, his prognosis. God was already and has always been Job's delight and worth. The suggestion that Job was simply longing for his wealth (v. 24) must have been further disheartening and proof again to Job that his friends did not understand his situation or him. Eliphaz says that in his restoration Job will pray to God and God will hear him (upon following Eliphaz's advice). In a wonderful twist of irony because Job did not follow Eliphaz's advice and give up his integrity, Job indeed did pray, this time for Eliphaz and the others (42:8), God did hear his prayer and they were delivered through the cleanness of his hands (v. 30).

Job's Eighth Speech (23:1-24:25)

23:1-7

Job is convinced that if he could get an audience with the Almighty then he would be vindicated and God would finish Job's suffering, but God is elusive.

Job, at this point, totally disregards all that Eliphaz has just said about him. He has already stated that his counsellors' attitudes toward him is one of mockery (21:3) and thus he continues to speak out of his suffering. While Job has confidence that a hearing would be to his benefit, he despairs of ever getting one (v. 3). Eliphaz has urged Job to turn to God (in repentance). Job, however, wishes to go a step further and state his case; as he has already said, why would he want such a thing unless he was innocent (13:14)?

23:8-12

Job's major issue is that no matter how devoted he has been he cannot get near to God.

With the use of metaphor, Job indicates that he has done all he can in order to find God so that he can put forth his case. Although Job cannot get to God, he is aware that God knows all about him and that a day will come when he will be vindicated because he has been a paragon of virtue, diligently seeking God for all the right reasons.

23:13-17

Job is certain that it is God (the One to which he is devoted) who is the author of his suffering and though in anguish he wants his 'day' with God.

Job, along with his friends, has held to the doctrine of retribution, however, his suffering has forced him to revaluate his worldview. His friends see no such need of re-evaluation and while Job does, he has no more firm conclusions, just questions to which he wants answers, but cannot obtain. Nothing is straightforward anymore, God is inscrutable. It is not just Job's understanding of God, nor his unimaginable and unfathomable suffering that is at stake, but also for the wise to be able to give answers to the big (and little) questions of life. Once Job's word was revered (29:21-23), now not only is he ridiculed, but he has no answers himself and this brings terror upon this man who has lost everything. However, despite God's seeming elusiveness, the turmoil that God has thrown upon Job and God's complete sovereignty to do as He wills, Job refuses to be silenced—the very thing his friends wish.

24:1-12

Job speaks of the great sins of men and asks why God does not judge them.

Job moves away from his own troubles to recognise that he is not the only person who suffers innocently. The question of theodicy, that is, God's governance of the world, is still in view, and does not receive a satisfying answer, as Job's story speaks to how to suffer innocently (cf. 1Pe 4:19), rather than why the innocent suffer. Unlike his friends, Job sees, in these examples at least, no time when God brings judgement on the wicked. The treatment of the vulnerable is an issue throughout the Scriptures and Job questions why people who abuse and exploit the vulnerable are not judged in this life when it is such a violation of God's principles (cf. Ex 22:22; Dt 19:14). Therefore, Job asks why God does not set aside specific days to act as Magistrate in order to deal with injustice? Job laments that those who know (and follow) his ways find the just judge absent.

The sins that Job outlines are similar to the sins that Eliphaz accuses Job of earlier; leaving people naked (22:6), not providing food and water for the needy (22:7) and being harsh towards widows and the fatherless (22:9). How could Job be so distressed at the treatment of society's vulnerable and be a perpetrator? His friends do not appear to appreciate the anomaly, but were saying by inference, "God is charging some with wrongdoing. God is charging you, Job!"

24:13-17

There are those who actively seek out the darkness in order to carry out their evil deeds.

Not only are there those who exploit the vulnerable, Job adds there are those who utterly reject God's truth (light, v. 13). The murderer, the adulterer, and the thief share a characteristic that is self-condemning: they all love darkness rather than the light (cf. 38:12-15; Ps 82:5). These evil deeds are usually done during the hours of darkness in order for darkness to cloak their activities; and therefore, darkness becomes their friend. This is a powerful symbol of the allegiance of the wicked, as true today as it was in Job's time.

24:18-24

Job acknowledges that even though the wicked are not judged by God they are nonetheless cursed and God is aware of their wrongdoing.

Some commentators do not attribute these words to Job, arguing that they sound so unlike him.[31] However, Job has never argued that the wicked always prosper nor never come to a bad end. Job's concern has been that God seems to treat the good and bad alike, which to Job is a great injustice. Job's concern is for the moral anomalies that occur and though God is aware, Job is

---

[31] For me, Elmer Smick makes sense when he says, "In addition to the difficulties in making sense of the text, there is the issue of determining whose words these are. Since there is no agreement, it seems wiser to let the text stand and above all refuse to force modern categories of logic and rhetoric on it." See, Smick, *Job*, *comment*, Job's reply, 23:1-24:25.

arguing that He does nothing.

24:25

Job asks his friends if what he has said is not true —
if it is true then their supposition, that the wicked
always get judged, is incorrect.

Surely Job's friends cannot deny that landmarks are
removed, widows robbed and the poor suffer want —
and the fact that such evils continue to happen is
apparent proof that God does nothing about it. In the
end the wicked die and are forgotten; they lack
security and have their day only for a little while
(22:16-18) — but, Job asks, where are the great days of
stored-up judgement so the righteous can be sure that
justice for such horrors is meted out? As Elmer Smick
suggests there is no direct teaching of final judgement,
but there is a concept here that anticipates the teaching
that God must have his day,[32] and the New Testament
teaching, in part, answers the issue of theodicy.

Bildad's Third Speech

25:1-6

Bildad counters Job's last argument by asserting
that no one is righteous before God and that proves
that Job must be wrong (24:25).

---

[32] Smick, *Job, comment* 24:25.

Bildad rushes to God's defence, proclaims God's order and rebuts Job's argument that the righteous and the wicked suffer the same by arguing that no one is righteous before God anyway (v. 4). The inference being that Job cannot claim righteousness or being unjustly treated; Job is getting what he deserves. However, Bildad does not come close to answering why even worse people don't suffer anything like Job has, unless as Eliphaz has said (22:5), that Job's wickedness is, indeed, great.

Job's Ninth Speech (26:1-31:40)

26:1-4

Job asks for Bildad's resume of care for the weak and suggests that his words come from a spiritual source behind Bildad.

Job has not been impressed by Bildad's last speech. Bildad has asserted that no one can be found blameless in God's sight; the ever present cry of Job, that he will be vindicated. Job resorts to sarcasm; Bildad, in fact has been no help at all. He has uttered the same words as Eliphaz (4:17) who claimed to have heard a, רוּחַ (*ruah*), spirit speak to him (4:15ff.), which presumably gave him insight. Job asks Bildad, whose נְשָׁמָה (*nᵉšāmâ*) spoke from his mouth? The NIV translates נְשָׁמָה (*nᵉšāmâ*) as spirit in only one other place; Proverbs 20:27 and therefore, this may be better translated, who put these words (breath) into your mouth? The answer, of course, is Eliphaz, and they are listening to the same רוּחַ (*ruah*) spirit.

26:5-14

Job describes the majesty of God's work on earth demonstrating God's rulership over the universe.

The thrust of these verses is that there is no place hidden from God; not just from His eye, but also His intervening power. The cosmic monsters of the sea (Rahab) and the air (gliding serpent), which Isaiah calls the fleeing serpent, Leviathan (Isaiah 27:1); Isaiah, rather than speaking in a primeval context as Job is, but in a future context with the deliverance of Israel — though different contexts are used the message is the same. Whatever these great forces may be, they are clearly reined in by God and as great and powerful as they are Job makes it clear that this is just the periphery of God's works. Therefore, when God comes close, who can understand Him? When God spoke to Jesus (Jn 12:28), some said it thundered. When the Apostle Paul had his Damascus Road experience, the men with him saw the light, but could not comprehend the sound (Ac 9:4; 22:9). Who then can comprehend God? Surely only to those whom God reveals Himself.

27:1-6

Job declares his innocence by an oath based on the existence of God.

Job continues his speech by making an oath based on the existence of God. In the culture of the day this is an extreme act; available as a last resort for a condemned person to plead innocent. This left only two possible considerations to be made concerning the condemned person; either he or she was innocent or a liar. If a liar, then he or she would suffer divine sanction for blaspheming God. This might not sound so extreme to modern readers, but was viewed with deep conviction in the ancient near east, and therefore, not done lightly. For Job to acknowledge that his friends were right in their assumptions about him meant that he has already condemned himself with his previous words. Not only would such a confession be untrue, it would then leave Job nowhere to turn; he is double damned. The man of integrity is left with only one option and that is to maintain his position of innocence; even on the pain of death.

27:7-10

Job calls down a curse upon those who would attack his innocence.

Job follows his oath by calling down a curse on his adversaries, which has dire consequences. This was no idle threat to the ancient mind. Sadly, by implication because Job's friends have accused him of being wicked, Job's curse falls on them. They have only spoken of God's justice and power, and not of His mercy, even though Job pleads for it (19:21). However, at the end of the story it isn't a curse that falls upon Job's friends, but instead mercy, as Job, at God's direction, prays for them (42:7-9).

27:11-23

Job gives a detailed description of the fate of the wicked.

Having just imprecated those who would attack his innocence, Job describes the fate of the wicked. This part of the speech is sometimes attributed to Zophar. However, Job has never denied that there is not a dire fate for the wicked, only that it is not absolutely true in this life. Just as he called his friends to observe and listen to what others have said about the prospering of the wicked (21:29 ff.), the opposite can also be observed. Much of what Job describes as the portion of the wicked is, here, pictured in terms of what has happened to his family, his wealth, and his own person. A wicked man's children, however many, are multiplied only for the sake of the sword or the plague (v. 14 f.), his wealth is left to others more righteous than himself (vv. 16-19), while he himself is carried off as if by flood, tempest or devastating east wind (vv. 20-23). This argument is a major reason for attributing this portion of speech to Zophar. However, taking the context of the whole speech and its climax with the dissertation on where wisdom is found (28:28), in my opinion, there is no reason to not attribute it to Job. Job's argument all along has been that there is rightly punishment for the wicked and he would agree that he is being punished in the manner of the wicked, as his friends argue. This is the nexus of the issue; Job is not wicked and is asking why he should be treated in this way.

Wisdom Poem (28:1-28)

Many biblical scholars do not attribute this poem regarding wisdom to Job. According to David Clines, "The consensus of scholarly opinion is that Ch. 28 is an independent poem, not set in the mouth of any of the speakers within the book of Job."[33] Although he, himself, attributes Chapter 28 to Elihu. If it were to be attributed to someone else, I would be inclined to attribute it to the narrator. If this portion of the book of Job has been misaligned there is no way of knowing how this happened, nor is there any sure indication that it actually has. It must be remembered that all the men in this drama ascribe to wisdom and are considered to be 'wise men', even if only in their own eyes (32:9; 34:2, 34) and are acutely aware of the collective wisdom of the age (8:8; 15:18). If these are the words of Job, and in my opinion there is no clear reason to think otherwise, they do fit with Job's quest for answers. The book is not simply a quest for answers to unjust suffering; to think that would be to deny the divine superintendence, which is so clearly

---

[33]David J. A. Clines, *Word Biblical Commentary: Job 21-37 on CD-ROM*, (Dallas: Word, 2002), comment 28:1-28.

stated in the prologue and God's intervention (chaps. 38-42). Wisdom is a primary theme; wisdom being founded in walking in the ways of Almighty God. It has been by wisdom that Job has guided his life, the problem being that it is not benefitting him in the midst of his great calamities (though previously it had). Though we need to bear in mind that the benefit of wisdom is only considered in terms prosperous living by the human characters. The question throughout the book is whether Job will abandon his piety, founded upon his wisdom, because it no longer secures for him a prosperous life or whether he will maintain it because it is the right way to live no matter what a person's circumstances. It is wisdom that is the driving motivation for Job's piety and as such there is no reason not to ascribe this portion of Job's last speech to the man himself.

28:1-11

Job outlines the lengths that men will go to in order to find things of value: precious stones, gold, silver.

Job begins this stanza with the length that men will go to in order to find what they consider to be precious. There is no shortage of archaeological evidence to support such mining practice.[34] Birds and proud beasts have no concern for such activities, nor do they see the value of precious stones and metals, but man labours intensely and intently for them.

---

[34] Smick, *Job, comment 28:1-11.*

Through such endeavour man brings these hidden things into the light of day (v. 11). Inherent in this stanza is the question as it appears in v. 12; what is the most precious? The answer being wisdom, which ought to be sought with the same diligence. Wisdom, like precious stones and metals, is hidden from the naked eye. Stones and metals need to be mined in order to bring them into the light; wisdom has to be lived in order for people to see it. Job has demonstrated his wisdom and was an honoured man; after his calamites, he still lived his wisdom, but was no longer honoured because men saw the fruit of wisdom in material prosperity, not in the integrity of one's relationship with God.

28:12-20

Wisdom cannot be found in the same place as precious stones and metals and though of more value, people do not comprehend its worth.

In the second stanza Job reveals the value he places on wisdom, the motivating energy behind his piety, but, sadly, despite its greater value, men prefer precious stones and metals. Clearly wisdom is not to be found in the same place as other valuables, nor is it seen to be as precious. Wisdom must be found elsewhere and no matter how precious these stones and metals are they cannot be used to buy wisdom and understanding. People may be clever, even ingenious and wealthy, but that does not mean that they are wise. Much later, Jesus makes the point regarding

God's view on what man considers precious (Lk 16:14f.); as a breath of fresh air, Job's great wealth had been no hindrance to his valuing what God valued.

28:20-28

God alone knows where wisdom and understanding can be found. To all but the omniscient the mine of wisdom is invisible.

If wisdom is so precious and cannot be found through ingenious human endeavour, where then can it be found? It is not tangible and, therefore, no living creature can see it; Death and Destruction only get a vague understanding. Only the omniscient God knows the way to it as Elmer Smick describes, "Wisdom is the summary of the genius God used to fashion the universe (cf. Pr 3:19-20)."[35] Wisdom is an attribute of God as Job has already stated (12:13) and while this cannot be mined there is a way for man to gain it. The climax of this poem gives the answer and the summary of Job's life; "The fear of the Lord—that is wisdom, and to shun evil is understanding." Therefore, acknowledging God, submitting to His ways and rejecting evil—that which God calls evil—is wisdom. Wisdom teaches a person how to live in a way that is pleasing to God and it is not only of temporal, but also of eternal benefit. When the temporal benefits seem few, as in Job's case during his suffering, the eternal benefits are beyond compare (1 Co 2:9).

---

[35] Smick, *Job*, comment 28:23-27.

Job's Summation (29:1-31:1-40)

Job concludes his speeches like a lawyer summing up his case. He presents three distinctive aspects which have been present throughout all his dialogues. In the first aspect (29:1-31) his mood is nostalgic where he recounts his former wealth, honour and happiness. The second (30:1-31) is bitter where Job laments his loss. Wealth is not his focus here, but his loss of dignity among men and friendship with God. With the third and last (31:1-40) he is more optimistic. He testifies with regard to both his inward attitude and outward behaviour, which have been pure, affirming to him that he has not been treated justly by God. Thus, like a prince (v. 37), he will approach God with dignity and self-assurance. He makes a series of oaths placing a curse upon himself which is to come into effect if he is being untruthful. Some of the curses would appear to have already fallen upon Job (others eating what he has sown [v. 8], physical ailment [v. 22]) and might be a self-defeating argument before his friends who believe that these are simply the results of being culpable. However, it is not to his friends that he presents this defence, but to God who knows.

Job is summoning God to a lawsuit and by means of reviewing his conduct Job gives himself a clean bill of health. He means to convince God that he is innocent of whatever charges God has against him. Job does not convince his friends though, who see this as part of his own sense of self-righteousness (32:1) and a denial of his own culpability. Clearly Job, like his friends, believes in the doctrine of retribution, though in numerous places Job has revealed that he is aware that the doctrine does not always hold true. Job, of course, is personalising the issue. While the doctrine might not always hold as inviolably as his friends perceive, why should it go against him? Job, and perhaps anybody else in a similar position, considers this to be a great wrong.

29:1-6

Job begins to wind up his case, like a lawyer at the end of a trial, with a reflection of his good days and a lament of his present.

Job begins his reflection with a recounting of his blessed days with God.

Job has no doubts about the source of his good life, though as the narrative reveals this was not reason for Job's piety. Job simply worshiped God as the natural response of the relationship between created and Creator. It is not surprising that Satan assumed Job's self-centred response because just as God allowed Satan to severely attack Job, to the opposite extent God had prospered him. Satan wanted to destroy Job beyond the suffering of all men, as God, it would seem, had prospered Job above all men. Job, though not a Hebrew, experienced intimate friendship with God (cf. 12:4) and he uses the hyperbole of his paths being drenched with cream and the rock pouring out streams of olive oil to express the incredible abundance he had received, perhaps even unnatural abundance.

29:7-17

The second aspect of Job's reflection on his good days focuses on the honour he had received among the community and how much of that was associated with his mercy toward the needy.

Not only was Job intimate with God and extremely prosperous, he was also an honoured man, deeply respected for his charity and his wisdom. It is true that in most societies, ancient and modern, that wealth makes a way into all manner of honoured situations and there is never a shortage of people who fawn after the wealth of others. There is also no shortage of unscrupulous wealthy people who court honour far beyond its due. Not so with Job. He has been accused of being a secret sinner; Eliphaz accused Job of not doing what Job is now claiming (22:5-7) and attributing Job's suffering to it. But Job now defends his care for the needy as it was his natural way of life flowing out of his relationship with God.

29:18-20

The third aspect of Job's reflection focuses on his previous hopes for the future.

Job had every good reason to expect that his good fortune would have continued to the end of his days, which he expected to be long. Sand is used frequently as a metaphor for a huge quantity (e.g., Ge 22:17; 32:12 [13]; Jos 11:4; Jdg 7:12; Ps 139:18; 39:18; in Job 6:3 it symbolizes weight). In a land where seasonal rains are scarce, a tree whose roots reach ground water and also receives the morning dew means more than mere survival in a harsh environment; the tree will flourish and that was Job's expectation. The key ingredient to Job's former life was honour (NIV glory) כָּבוֹד (*kābôd*), to which Ch. 29 attests, and was received primarily because of his relationship with God. The twist of irony in this, is that what Job had hoped for, now seemingly lost to him, is exactly what he receives after his restoration.

29:21-25

In the fourth aspect of Job's reflection, he returns to the honour he had received, with good reason, among men.

To what extent others had seen Job in the same light as he saw himself we cannot know for sure. It would seem clear that he was not a tyrannical ruler who demanded respect on the pain of death, but was honoured for his wisdom, social concern and the influence of his prosperity which would benefit those around him. Job would have been exactly the type of person a community would want to have as its chief (v. 25). With no blemish or hint of corruption the people could 'sleep easy'. Job was a godlike character, perhaps like Melchizedek (Ge 14:18). His counsel was valued, his approval was sought and his leadership accepted with gratitude. Job had fallen from being honoured by all to being despised by all. His previous life and good work has not counted in his favour at all now, even though he had done nothing to deserve such treatment.

30:1-8

Though once honoured by all, now Job is despised, even by the lowliest.

Previously, the highest level of society held Job in the highest respect (29:9-10) and kept silent when he spoke. That is now contrasted with the lowest level of society who mock and detest him.

30:9-15

Not only is Job mocked, but the lowest level of society consider themselves superior to him and Job has no power to stop it.

Job had expected days of continual flourishing (29:18-20). The bow, a symbol of strength to be forever in his hand has now been unstrung by God and for this reason alone Job is no longer able to protect himself. It would seem that it was the natural inclination for these people to attack Job, but they could not do so in Job's previous God-given strength and prosperity. But since God has taken that away they rush in against him. It is not unusual for the disenfranchised in any society to despise the prosperous; to wish them ill and steal from them. Now that Job is a powerless and afflicted man they can vent their jealous rage against him.

30:16-23

Adding to his abasement, Job's life, once expected to be long, is coming to an end and God continues to humiliate him more.

Job now turns his attention back to his sufferings and his God who is the cause of it all. Not only is he gripped by suffering (v. 16), but God constricts his life like a garment choking the neck, throwing the helpless man into the mud to reduce him to nothing. Dust and ashes were the remains of rubbish and is the perfect metaphor for how Job perceives himself in the eyes of both God and man. Previously, Job had 'intimate friendship' with God (29:4-5), but Job perceives through his circumstances that the friendship has 'turned sour'. The irony being that in men's eyes that is indeed how he is considered, but not by God, to which all men (including Job) are blinded.

30:24-31

Convention suggests that further degradation is withheld from those in deep distress, but not so for Job; there is no end to his suffering and no help forthcoming.

The very kindness he had so freely given, he now looks for in vain. Verse 26 reminds us of his expectations expressed in 29:18-20, but the opposite has come to pass. Consequently, Job reiterates his disgrace in the eyes of men, with which he began this speech where he is considered no better than wild creatures (v. 29). His skin disease is a cause for further loathing and the (happy) music of his former life has been turned to mourning. It is difficult to imagine a person in such abject despair or a life that can be contrasted so starkly. It is also hard to imagine that a righteous man would be treated this way by men or by God, not only for the reader, but also the victim himself. Job is about to end his speech with an exposition of his righteous life, but before he does, his suffering and hopelessness leaves the reader breathless.

31:1-4

Job knows there is no escape from God's gaze and judgement comes to those who do evil, therefore, even in his contemplation he would not drift into evil thoughts, in this case citing sexual lust.

Job is aware that all he does is seen by God and with this sense of constant divine vigilance he knows that there is nothing he can 'get away' with. Thus he orders his life with discipline with the intention that fleshly concerns do not take hold. The first concern that Job raises is sexual lust. The term is בִּין (*bîn*), meaning to 'consider, contemplate'; this does not mean that Job has compelled himself to look away every time he sees a young woman. In Job's culture there was nothing wrong with men, even married men, looking with pleasure, delight, longing, or even lust upon young women. It was considered necessary if a man of Job's social standing was ever going to attain a second wife or concubines.[36] Generally, it is not considered wrong in modern life either. Jesus, however, made the issue very clear in Matthew 5:28 and thus we get God's view of sexual lust, and Job, long before the Sermon on the Mount, knew what was right in this area of life and thus made a covenant with his eyes (v. 1). He knew God was watching and judges evil.

31:5-8

Job's second area of self-defence is the honesty with which he approached life, particularly business, and he calls down a curse upon himself if he has been deceitful as proof of his integrity.

In a modern world where talk is cheap and written contracts can be set aside or changed,[37] an oath made to declare integrity carries little value. Not so in the ancient world, as Elmer Smick puts it; "In Job's world there were no atheists or even secularists. Everyone believed in the validity of divine sanction. This made the oath the ultimate test of integrity."[38] In this second area of self-defence Job focuses on honesty; presumably he has in mind his commercial activities. He has not deceived people nor has he allowed his

---

[36]Clines, *Job 21-37*, comment 31:1.
[37] See Gal 3:15 for the ancient view of contracts or covenants.
[38] Smick, *Job*, comment 31:5-8.

eyes to lead him (cf. Nu 15:39). Job is certain that if weighed on God's scales he would be found innocent of such wrongdoing and calls down the curse of not eating from the labour of his hands if he is guilty. Others, of course, would have eaten what he had sown after Satan's attack, but Job knows he is innocent.

31:9-12

The third aspect of Job's self-defence is his blamelessness with regard to adultery.

In verse 1 Job speaks of adultery of the heart; here in his third aspect of self-defence he speaks to the issue of physically committing adultery, which he denies ever doing. Some may seek to justify such sin, but Job not only calls down a curse upon himself if he has done such a thing, but he asserts that such an act would be shameful and, indeed, deserving of punishment. In Mosaic Law adultery was a capital offense (cf. Lev 20:10); here Job invokes the 'eye for an eye' justice upon his wife if he has committed adultery. Job recognises that adultery is not a self-contained or containable incident, but the initiation of a process of annihilation. This can be graphically seen in king David's life after committing adultery with Bathsheba (2Sa 11:3). Inherent in the act of adultery is destructive evil, of which righteous Job would have no part.

31:13-15

The fourth aspect of Job's self-defence is his attitude and response to his slaves who he considers also to have rights and are as much human as he is — created by the same God.

Job has not regarded his servants, most likely slaves, as mere chattels, as was the common attitude in Ancient Near Eastern culture. Though he has not gone so far as to emancipate them, he has treated them in an egalitarian fashion in that he recognises that they have the same origin (v. 15). Job adds that his slaves have rights, even when the grievance was against him. The basis of his attitude is found in his belief that he must give an account of his actions to his moral God.

31:16-23

The fifth aspect of Job's self-defence relates to his social conscience and he affirms that he has taken care of the widow, the orphan and the poor, motivated by his fear of God.

Job has been accused of abuses toward the vulnerable in society by Eliphaz (22:6-9) and has defended his social conscience (29:12-17). Here, as if to settle the issue, he reiterates his concern for the vulnerable in society by an oath in which Job calls a curse upon himself if he has failed in this respect. The curse of punishment that Job invites upon himself parallels literally what he could do metaphorically, that is, lift his hand against the fatherless. The curse of his hand along with his arm falling from his shoulder (v. 22), carries the image of breaking the man's strength. Job's motivation is founded upon the dread of God's punishment—his fear of the Lord is real (28:28). In a modern world and even in a modern church the fear of the Lord is something to equate to awesome reverence. However, for Job, the fear of the Lord is more than that—it makes a man tremble, especially for the destruction God can bring upon a man. Jesus reiterated this concept in Luke 12:4-5. Since the Charismatic renewal of the 1960s and 70s, a common focus of the church's relationship with God is as with a friend. The image of God given is of a friend with similar standing to the person, perhaps of an older friend or older brother and this, of course, dispels the frightening image of a wrathful God before whom people ought to fear and tremble.

As with many errors of the church, this image of God as our friend (almost equal) is an overemphasised truth. Jesus surely can be envisioned as an older brother by those who receive Him (Jn 1:12), but not an older brother as within usual familial relationships because Jesus is exalted to the highest place (Phil 2:9-11; Col 1:15-20; Rev 3:14). His goal is to present us before the Father in a way in which the Father is well pleased; Jesus is Lord. God the Father can also be considered our friend; He works to reconcile humanity to Himself. However, the idea of the friend here is not one of mutual relation, rather God the Father being kindly disposed toward mankind as our loving Creator; there can be no sense of mutuality. The Holy Spirit also can be considered our friend for He is the 'paraclete'; the One who walks beside. But this too is not a friendship found in mutuality, but one where the

Spirit of God would guide the child of God into the will of God. Job clearly has a living relationship with God, and he has certainly not lost sight of the wrath of God that befalls the rebellious and this is the reason for the sober way he walked in the world before men.

31:24-28

The sixth aspect of Job's self-defence is in relation to idolatry, in which Job swears that not even in his heart has he been unfaithful to God.

Perhaps when all religious worship is stripped bare, outside of the faithful worship of God, the worship of mammon will certainly almost always be found (cf. Mt 6:24; Lk 16:13) because wealth takes the material struggle from life. Job, who was exceedingly wealthy and had what so many dreamed of and envied, could have easily allowed his trust to slip from God to gold. No doubt he was thankful for his great wealth, but his thanks went to God through whom the wealth came, not the wealth itself. Neither did Job engage in the popular astral worship either. As a form of sun and moon worship the practice of throwing kisses was practiced. Job clearly considers such an attitude of trust, worship and devotion apart from God to be wickedness (sins) deserving judgement; again through these statements as before, Job is declaring in the strongest terms that he has not done so.

31:29-34

The seventh aspect of Job's self-defence relates to

his attitude toward other people; fear of enemies, strangers and the crowd—towards all of which he has acted in genuine godliness.

Just as so much stripped back religion reveals the worship of mammon, so too, much of human interrelationships can be stripped back to fear. It is common to fear an enemy and to gloat over his misfortune. It is not unusual to fear strangers and, therefore, not practice hospitality. It is also common to fear the crowd and go along with the mob; a behaviour graphically evidenced during an election when a political party is polling badly. Job's interrelationships were not founded on the fear of men, but of God, which meant he could act in love toward people and fulfil the second greatest command because he fulfilled the first (cf. 1Jn 4:18-21).

31:35-37

With his self-defence definitively assured, Job believes that he can now stand before God and hear God's accusation because he is certain that he will be found innocent.

As Job has recounted his moral life he has become so assured of his innocence that he invites God to put His accusations against him, believing that God would have nothing of which to accuse him; Job could wear God's indictment as a crown. Needless to say his friends see this as being righteous in his own eyes (32:1), but Job has so talked himself up that he now feels capable of facing God as a prince or ruler indignant of being wrongly charged. Despite the truth of his morality, his conviction in his ability to stand before God will later melt (42:4-6). In similar fashion was Peter's great vow before Jesus (Mt 26:35). Solid conviction before the fact is easy to muster, but in the face of conflict it can easily dissolve into empty bluster. Job was right with regard to his morality and the pious nature on which his morality was founded, but even his charge of being wrongly accused gets no hearing and he finds that, indeed, he cannot approach God. He needs the advocate of whom he previously spoke (16:19); one who would represent him, as the Christian has Christ. But now, at the end of his final speech, he is brimming with self-confidence.

31:38-40

Job's eighth, and final appeal in his self-defence is found in his treatment of the land and the people who work the land for him; he is sure there can be no complaint against him.

As the blood of Abel cried out of the ground (Ge 4:10) so can the land cry out to God for any oppression or exploitation, as can Job's workers if he is guilty. Job is sure that the land will not and thus, in full confidence he calls down the ancient curse upon his land (Ge 3:18). Job is assured of his complete innocence, his friends cannot convince him otherwise, and thus there is now nothing more to say to them.

Elihu's Speeches (32:1-37:24)

Elihu is from the tribe of Buz (cf. Ge 22:21), a kindred tribe to Uz (1:1). Uz and Buz were brothers. Although younger than Job, perhaps he was not unknown to him. His lineage is through Abraham's brother, Nahor, therefore he has the family status entitling him to speak. It would appear then, that he too, along with the other characters, is an Edomite. His theology is more balanced than the other three counsellors' and he has paid more attention to Job's arguments, even quoting his words. In the process of validating his right to speak, he comes across as sanctimonious and long winded. In his favour he does not limit God's punishment to condemnation, but introduces the idea that God punishes as a disciplinary act of mercy in order for the punished to repent and be restored. He applies this theology to Job and while it certainly has a place, and Israel's history clearly attests to this principle, it is, however, misplaced in Job's case and, thus, is no comfort to Job.

Elihu was angry with Job's friends for their inability to convince Job of his need to repent and angry with Job because Elihu considered him to be self-righteous. In the end, though, he does no better in convincing Job of his sinfulness. Elihu is not mentioned in the epilogue (42:7-9) and it would appear that God was not as angry with him as with the other three. No adequate explanation can be given for this. However, God's condemnation of the three was directly attributed to how they had spoken of Him (42:7-8). In their defence of God against Job they had misrepresented God, and Elihu does not make that error in the same way. His argument that God was bringing Job to repentance was not entirely wrong either, because that is how Job finally responds to God, and so, perhaps this is why Elihu is not mentioned in the epilogue. In the end though, he too failed to comprehend Job's situation as presented in the prologue—that Job was suffering as a chosen servant to the ultimate glory of God, which exposed Satan as the false accuser that he was.

32:1-5

The younger man Elihu is introduced into the story and he is angry with Job for his apparent self-righteousness, and also Job's friends because they could not convince Job of his need to repent, and so he seeks to bring Job to repentance and restoration.

At the end of Job's final speech the narrator introduces the character, Elihu. His relationship to Job is unknown (but it is certainly possible that Job did know of Elihu given the closeness of their family tribes). It is questionable if he can even be called a friend, especially as Elihu is so much younger. However, he is given the privilege of speaking where he rebukes both Job's friends and Job himself, which indicates that he is a young man of no small stature. In his speeches he desires to exalt the Lord, which is fitting as his name means God is Lord, but his drive to speak is born of anger, and like many zealous God-fearing young people, courtesy is pushed aside for the blunt instrument of truth as he understands it and thus he gives vent to the errors he sees in the older generation. His desire, as with the others, is not to harm Job, but to help him and see his restoration, believing that where the others failed, he will succeed. And so, like the others, Elihu believes Job's restoration can only come as he accepts his 'good' advice and puts it into practice.

32:6-9

Elihu has shown deference to the older men, waiting to speak, and now with his opportunity he wants to show that he too has wisdom, given to him by God.

Elihu has shown the customary deference while listening to the older men. All that he has heard has caused him to become angry as he believes Eliphaz, Bildad, and Zophar have missed the point of Job's suffering. He begins by building a case for a legitimate right to speak using his premise that wisdom is not only found among the older generation, but that God can give it to the young and, indeed, has given, even superior wisdom to him. In effect, Elihu is saying that God is speaking through him.

32:10-14

Speaking to Job's friends, Elihu rebukes them for not having an adequate answer for Job, which he will now address.

Elihu's motivation to speak is driven by the friends' failure to prove Job wrong. He speaks to them bluntly asserting that their arguments were inherently weak and thus he will not use them. The idea that the friends are now leaving Job in God's hands (v. 13) is infuriating to Elihu, and he believes he has the answer to Job's problem.

32:15-22

Elihu feels compelled to speak the bare truth without fear or favour.

Elihu continues with his wordy defence for his participation in the conversation and he is true to himself when he says he is full of words (v. 18). Such is his compulsion to speak he feels as if he will burst if he does not. One might be able to sense his fidgeting frustration as he listened to the previous speeches, itching to butt in but restrained by convention. He declares that he is impartial (v. 21) and that he will talk straight, implying that Job must brace himself for what is about to come.

33:1-7

Elihu declares the foundation upon which his right to speak rests; he is upright, sincere and made in the image of God.

Aware that Job has lost all confidence in the sincerity of his friends (cf. 12:2; 13:4-5; 16:2-5; 19:2-6, 28-29; 21:3, 34; 26:1-4), Elihu stresses the sincerity of his intent. It would seem that Elihu considers himself superior in understanding to Job and does not expect Job to be able to refute him as he did the others. Not wanting to press his sense of superiority, Elihu affirms that he is a man like Job and Job need not fear him in the way that Job has feared the hand of God (cf. 6:4; 13:21; 18:11; 30:15). Elihu sees himself in the role of the mediator that he spoke of in 33:23; all the straight talking that he is about to do is going to be for Job's good.

33:8-12

Elihu has been listening and reflects Job's complaints; that although Job is pure and without guilt God has found him guilty.

Elihu fairly accurately and succinctly reflects Job's complaint (cf. 13:24b and 27a).

Although Job has not quite claimed sinlessness (7:21; 10:6; 13:26), in Job's speeches his complete innocence is the tenor. This could easily be misconstrued by Elihu as sinlessness and that is the issue Elihu wants to address. Very matter of factly, Elihu, in his defence of God, declares that Job is wrong.

33:13-22

One of Job's complaints has been that God will not speak to him; Elihu implies that God is speaking to Job through his suffering.

Elihu now picks up on Job's complaint that God will not give him a hearing (cf. 9:16, 35; 13:22; 19:7;

23:2-7). Job has been requesting a one-on-one meeting (cf. 13:15), however, Elihu elaborates on how God might speak to mankind. He suggests that God will speak through dreams and visions, even speak words into a man's ears. Elihu gets very pointed when he asserts that another way God will speak to a man is by causing him to suffer, and then he describes Job's symptoms. According to Elihu, the purpose for God speaking was to warn (v. 16) and to discipline (v. 19). The inference for Job is that he is being disciplined by God because he deserves it. Job does not need to be told that he is being disciplined by God; he knows that only too well. Elihu, like the other friends, thought the reason was obvious and completely dismisses Job's protestations to the contrary.

33:23-30

According to Elihu, Job's suffering is God's way of being merciful so that Job would take stock, repent and have his life restored.

Elihu introduces the faint possibility (one in a thousand [v. 23]) of a mediating angel that might speak on behalf of the suffering in order that the suffering might find mercy and not the justice their deeds deserve. According to Elihu, the purpose of suffering, then mediation, is to bring a person to restoration upon which repentance and thanksgiving come. This idea goes beyond Eliphaz, Bildad and Zophar's wisdom who see only **judgement** in suffering. For Elihu, suffering is an issue of **mercy,** not so that Job can be accused, but to be cleared. Though Job does not speak, consistent with his other speeches he would likely be asking, "Cleared of what?"

33:29-33

Elihu commands Job to listen to his superior wisdom, given for his benefit.

Elihu moves from the possibility of mediating mercy (v. 23) to the patience of God where He will act in mercy two or three times (v. 29) in order to restore a person. There are elements of what Elihu says that fit with the ministry of Christ, but taken as a whole he severely limits God's grace. Elihu is convinced, however, of his insight and his benevolent attitude toward Job (v. 32). Job had said to his friends that for them wisdom would be to 'shut up' (13:5) because Job has lived by wisdom founded in God's words (28:28), but Elihu, the younger, will now proceed to teach Job wisdom. He has become the self-appointed teacher because the other men have been unable to refute Job and Job, because of his suffering, appears to be the one who needs to learn. In any case, more education on the theory of suffering is of little benefit to the sufferer, especially when the sufferer is powerless to do anything about it.

34:1-4

Elihu invites all who are wise to join him in his banquet of words to find out how good they (that is, his words) are.

Elihu now addresses the other men as well (possibly bystanders who are listening); he is not going to just be Job's teacher, but theirs too. What Elihu means by, "let us learn together what is good" is not a work of collaboration or symposium where minds might meet and discuss, but rather to listen to his wisdom and learn from it.

34:5-9

In order to build his case against Job, that Job is in need of repentance, Elihu begins his dissection of Job's character; here a blasphemer and an associate of evildoers.

Elihu at least quotes Job's words, which is more that the others had done, however, he uses them against Job and appeals to his listeners to consider whether they have come across one like Job, who blasphemes as easily as drinking water (v. 7). Not only that, Job keeps the company of the wicked. Eliphaz has said that humans are naturally disposed to drinking evil like water (15:16), and Job is among them. Nowhere has Job suggested that he keeps the company of the wicked, rather the opposite (21:16). He has simply asked how does it profit a man to be righteous when the righteous and wicked get treated alike (9:22; 21:7)? From this Elihu has concluded that Job has given up his life of pleasing God.

Restoration through legalism or grace?

There is a subtle sense here for Elihu and the other three that the worship of God is founded on a judicial basis—a prescribed way of living with its concomitant rewards and punishment (bearing in mind that the characters in this story are unlikely to be living under Mosaic Law). The church has a tendency to be legalistic also and confine the worship of God to following a series of rules or principles. Notwithstanding that there are rules and principles, these are not to be the foundation on which the Christian life is built. Rather, the foundation is the new birth—born of God into a new family (Jn 1:12-13), dead to one kingdom and alive to another (Gal 1:4; Eph 2:1ff; Col 1:13). With divine parentage new Christians absorb the values and the life of the kingdom of God because they are, by the power of the Spirit, if engaged, becoming like their Father in heaven, as Jesus modelled on earth.

Within the family of God there is correction, there is also reward. This is the case with any family, necessary to keep the growing child close to the fidelity of the family values to which they belong. Correction is not meant to banish or exclude, but used in order to include and maintain relationships (cf. Heb 12:4-11). Correction within the kingdom of God has its roots in restoration—disciplinary actions are meant for mercy leading towards repentance. Such an idea has been regularly misused in the hands of the religiously self-righteous, however, in righteous hands the principle is sound. If the Christian desires to develop the image of God in which he or she has been created, correction is seen as positive (helpful if administered positively) and is meted out, not for the purposes of vengeance or anger against wrongdoing, but for the purposes of guidance. The idea is to bring the person back into the values (worldview) from which, by their action (or inaction), they have stepped away.

Job's disciplined world has fallen apart and few suffer the calamity that he did. Much of what he believed about life now appears to be wrong. If he were to keep the company of evildoers when in the past he would not (vv. 8-9), it is not because he intends to do evil, but to look for answers. However, such an argument (34:8) is moot because Job already stated that he stands aloof from the counsel of the wicked (21:16). Job had previously subscribed to the worldview of his friends and lived a disciplined life, perhaps more out of the fear of God than love of Him, but now he cannot hold to it anymore; the legalistic mindset and the disciplined life do not seem to hold true anymore. Hence, the issue of Job is not why the good suffer, but how the righteous live in that suffering. It wasn't just his friends whose mindsets needed expanding, Job's did too. Arguably, the church needs constant encouragement to expand her understanding of the way of righteousness (Mt 22:16). Elihu intends to do this with his audience, but will fail; the church has the word of God and His Spirit to give interpretation, yet also often fails, not because God is limited, but because we are limited. Thus, perhaps, the rule of thumb in dealing with people, which Job's friends failed to do, is to err on the side of grace rather than legalism, with restoration always in mind.

34:10-15

Elihu expounds his conventional theology; the sovereignty of God, the doctrine of retribution and God's non-accountability to His creation.

Job had complained "that those who provoke God are secure" (12:6) while one who is "righteous and blameless" is made "a laughing stock" (12:4; cf. 10:3; 21:7-8; 24:1-12). To Elihu this could only mean that Job is charging God with wrongdoing, something which he could not accept. Elihu is not alone in this view, Job also held to it, however, Elihu misunderstands Job's question and therefore expounds on the greatness of God and states the conventional form of the doctrine of retribution (v. 11). Therefore, in Elihu's mind, like the others, Job's circumstances prove his wickedness.

34:16-20

Elihu argues that the government of the universe cannot be presumed to be unrighteous and judges according to righteousness.

Elihu turns now to Job and addresses him directly,[39]

---

[39]Clines, *Job 21-37*, comment 34:16. The imperative verbs "hear" שְׁמַע (*šāma*') and "give ear" (NIV listen) אַזִן [hiph] (*'āzan)* in the singular show that Elihu is now addressing Job directly.

continuing with his theme of God being the universal ruler who cannot act wrongly; any suggestion to the contrary by Job is itself an act of wickedness. Elihu strongly believes he is right and, therefore, if Job has any understanding he will listen and see that Elihu is right. In this section of speech Job is certain to agree with Elihu's exposition of the sovereignty of God who has the power to judge kings and nobles; Job has already said similarly (12:17ff.).

34:21-30

Elihu continues to elaborate on God's righteous governorship, ensuring that corrupt leaders are dealt with.

Job has pleaded for a hearing before God (9:15; 13:3; 23:4,7). Elihu asserts that this is unnecessary because God is already aware of the actions of men and judges without the need of further inquiry. Even if God is silent He still watches over individuals as well as nations to ensure that righteousness prevails. Elihu's primary concern is with God's justice concerning the mighty and as Job was a significant community leader (29:25) then Elihu is making the point that Job is being justly treated and his complaints are invalid.

34:31-33

God will accept the repentant, but as Elihu and the others perceive that Job is unrepentant, they believe that God cannot accept him.

The only way forward for Job, according to Elihu, is to acknowledge his sin and promise to not do so again. But because of Job's self-righteous stance (32:1) there can be no hope for Job (v. 33) and thus, Elihu adds rebellion (v. 37).

34:34-37

Elihu declares that Job is not only ignorant, but increases his sin by defending himself in the manner he has.

Elihu wants Job to be cleared of God's judgement upon his life (33:32) but because Job has refused to accept the counsel of the other friends Elihu appears to feel the need to speak strongly and certainly without any flattery (cf. 32:22). In this quest for truth each party has accused the other of ignorance (cf. 18:1-4; 32:3) and Elihu is no exception. Not that Job has responded to anything Elihu has said, but Elihu speaks as though Job has rejected his words and wants further testing to come upon Job (v. 36). According to Elihu, it would seem that in God's merciful judgement, what Job has already suffered has been insufficient to bring him to repentance, but instead made him more of a sinner and, therefore, more suffering is required. In other words, Job must be broken.

How can Job be accused of the sin of rebellion? Elihu's accusation rests in his worldview that evil acts are always punished and, therefore, if a person, like Job, is suffering, the *only* conclusion that can be drawn is that Job is wicked. If that worldview is deeply held, and that appears to be the case, Job saying that in his case it is not so, could only be understood as being rebellious. The reader, of course, has greater insight than all the characters because of their glimpse into the heavenly council and, therefore, knows that Job is not suffering because of his sin, but because of his righteousness. While God is sovereign, He has given licence to Satan, and it is this evil hand that has brought the suffering upon Job, though the reader might not immediately be aware of God's purpose in allowing it. What the reader can be sure of is that Elihu is falsely accusing Job, and hopefully will appreciate the danger of misapplying simple theology, filtered through a cultural worldview, to a person's circumstances. It is all too easy to draw wrong conclusions about people and their circumstances; Jesus' warning about making such judgements are pertinent here (cf. Mt 7:1; Lk 6:37).

35:1-3

Elihu accuses Job of suggesting that he is no better off than if he had sinned and that there is no benefit in righteousness; Job has not said this.

Elihu misunderstands Job's position and believes that Job has said that he would gain nothing by not sinning. Job has not said this at all, but has made the observation that there are times when the wicked prosper and times when the righteous suffer. In 21:1-16 Job speaks of the prosperity of the wicked, and ends by declaring that he will avoid such company. Elihu certainly is a man of wisdom, but he has no comprehension of Job's situation yet, believing that he does, is certain that Job is deluding himself if Job thinks he can be cleared by God without repentance. It is Elihu's expressed desire to see Job cleared, but expressly on his terms.

35:4-8

Elihu declares that neither sinfulness nor righteousness has any effect upon God; He neither benefits nor suffers—only humanity is impacted.

For Elihu, the transcendence of God is so far above humanity that He cannot be affected by human behaviour. The righteousness or wickedness of human beings only affects other human beings.[40] Job has not helped his case by asking God, "If I have sinned what have I done to you?" (7:20), but Elihu does not seem to have an understanding of the imminence of God in the same way Job has (12:4b; 17:17-20). It could be said that Elihu knows more about God than actually knows God.

35:9-16

Elihu assumes that Job cannot get a hearing from God because he, like others who suffer, holds onto his wickedness; such cries (for justice) come to God as the

---

[40] Elihu makes no comment on the benefits or otherwise of human behaviour on the environment.

sound of a brute beast.

Elihu addresses the issue of why Job and others are not delivered from their suffering; in essence, because those suffering will not acknowledge God. Elihu's doctrine is that God sends suffering as an act of mercy in order to bring restoration and repentance, without which suffering cannot end. Instead of crying out to God, the oppressed cry out to powerful people. Job might not be one of the wicked, but to Elihu, he shares in their arrogance and in his rebellious spirit (34:37) admonishes God for hiding His face (13:24; 23:8-9; cf. v. 14), and wants to march into God's presence as an impatient litigant (13:15; 31:35-37). To Elihu, Job can never get an answer from God; in fact he thinks Job should be further tested (34:36), and chides Job for speaking empty words as have Bildad (8:2; 18:2) and Eliphaz (15:2-3) before him.

36:1-4

Elihu believes that he is doing God a service by defending Him against Job and confidently posits himself as being right (v. 4).

Aware that he has been speaking for some time Elihu politely asks for patience as he begins to finish his speech. In his thinking they should want to listen because he considers himself to have perfect understanding. Elihu seeks to invite Job to stop his complaint against God and marvel at divine justice, God's self-revelation, and perhaps most importantly,

God's mercy, which Job could so easily receive. Elihu is convinced of the accuracy of his understanding; this is more than his sincere opinion. Elihu has built a case for the justice and mercy of God in order that Job would respond and be cleared of his unrighteousness and thus, his suffering cease. Elihu can do this because he considers himself to be superior in his knowledge of God's ways. He can easily convince himself of this as he understands an aspect of God's mercy that Eliphaz, Bildad and Zophar did not entertain. Adding to his view is Job's suffering, the cause being self-evident to Elihu, and on top of all this he believes his words are derived from God. The young man's motives are sincere (33:3) as were the others', but sincerity of heart is of no help at all when the premise on which an argument is built is wrong.

36:5-12

Elihu restates his doctrine of suffering as discipline in order for the unrighteous to turn back to God and find prosperity.

Elihu speaks with sweeping generalities, seeking to apply generality to Job's specific circumstance. He declares that God is clear in His dealings with men and has the might to carry out His purposes, which are exalted. He affirms the conventional understanding that the wicked get judgement in order for the afflicted to get their rights, but adds that God continually watches over the righteous who exalt Him. Still considering the righteous, Elihu speaks of their suffering as divine discipline for wrongdoing (cf. 33:15-30), which is a merciful act on God's part, giving suffering as an opportunity to cry out to God and thus receive mercy. Repentance is available according to Elihu, and he is making an allowance for people who have not become hardened by their wickedness. However, if they do not listen to God (speaking to them through their suffering) they will perish, and that before their time (v. 14).

36:13-14

Elihu turns his attention to the godless of heart, the unrepentant—they who reject God's chastisement will die in shame.

Elihu's theological position is that God is using Job's misery in order to win him back to righteous living. Now, not content with using generalities he goes on to add hyperbole, saying that if those suffering do not respond to God then they will die in the greatest of shame. Prostitutes were (and are) perhaps among the most despised members of society, and to end up as a male shrine prostitute was arguably the lowest social position; obviously it is the shameful end of the wicked that is Elihu's point. The veiled message is that this will be Job's fate if he does not take heed of Elihu's counsel and repent.

36:15-21

Elihu reiterates his theological position that God is using Job's misery in order to win him back to righteous living.

After speaking generally, Elihu now speaks directly to Job again and seeks to further enlighten him—Job is in a desperate situation because God has judged his wickedness. He warns Job to not act wickedly and cites examples of wickedness, warning Job to avoid the evil Elihu believes Job is inclined towards. Because Job has cited how the godless can prosper, Elihu is fearful that Job might take that option. Clearly, he has misunderstood Job—Job's point has been that even if the wicked prosper that is not a path he would walk upon. Elihu might be sincere, but he is, on this point, sincerely wrong. It is a good time to be reminded that God called Job righteous.

36:22-26

In expounding the glorious righteousness of God in all that Elihu has just said (vv. 1-21), he voices a hymn of praise to God.

God is exalted in His power and who teaches like God? Elihu wants Job to reflect on this, stop complaining, accept what God has said about him (evidenced through his circumstances) and focus on God's power and wisdom.

36:27-33

Elihu continues his hymn of praise speaking of the majesty of God.

Elihu underscores God's greatness evidenced in the

water cycle. Rain is one of the most needed and obvious blessings from God, but it can also be destructive (storm and lightning) and it is one means of expressing judgement between people (v. 31a). All that is said is designed to give Job a sense of God's greatness and worth-ship to help convince him to turn back to God.

37:1-13

Elihu rejoices in the majesty and power of God over the forces of nature which bring both blessing and punishment to men as appropriate, and through this, men will know God's work (v. 7).

Elihu continues to draw upon the marvels of nature to illustrate his argument of God's sovereign hand over human affairs. Elihu perceives the living presence of God in the thunder and lightning (cf. Hab 3:6) and states that God sends the snow and the rain in order for men to know of His work. Thus His control of nature and His presence within is to bless or to punish.

37:14-18

Elihu invites Job to consider sovereign majesty and realise how insignificant he is.

Elihu makes the point that Job is insignificant in comparison with God's power and control. Using rhetorical questions, he drives home his message that Job has no conception of how God controls the forces of nature; Job cannot know God's ways. The inference being that Job has no right to question God; in essence, according to Elihu, Job is being absurd.

37:19-24

Elihu finishes by declaring to Job that though humanity can rest assured that God is exalted in both power and justice, God is beyond human reach and, therefore, Job should simply fear God and become wise.

Job has argued for an audience with God, however, Elihu says that that is impossible; human beings cannot speak to God because they are in darkness (v. 19). He reiterates his previous premise that God is beyond human interaction, but from a distance forever watching, God dispenses justice, acting righteously toward men. Elihu's final statement is to call all men to revere (fear) the God that he has described because God looks with favour upon those who are wise.

The conclusion that Elihu has drawn is that Job has not been truly wise, rather wise in his own eyes and until Job repents, turns to God and understands God according to Elihu's insight, Job will continue to suffer.

Yahweh Speaks (38:1-41:34)

38:1-3

Job, considered to be a wise man, is now addressed by God by means of a series of questions which confirm Job's limited wisdom.

Elihu has spoken of the presence of God in the storm and it is out of the storm that God speaks. Job has longed for his day with God, he has prepared his case (13:18; 31:35) and believes that he will be vindicated. God addresses him as being without knowledge, though from a human perspective he had been considered to be a man of wisdom. As have so many, Job has asked questions of God because God's actions upon him do not fit with his understanding of God's moral application of justice. Job, in his poetic rage, thinks that God considers him an enemy (13:24; 33:10). This consideration is founded in the great suffering he faces believed to be an act of punishment from God. However, Job has no idea of why he is being punished. It was from God and God alone that Job believed his vindication would come. As he now stands before God he needs to brace himself. He has imagined things about God and it could be said that much of his speech was directed to a god largely of his own imagination because his conception of God's motive and actions against him were not the reality. Job, now, faces God as He really is.

God cannot always be nailed down by neat theological doctrines and speaking through the prophet Isaiah God says, *"For my thoughts are not your thoughts, neither are your ways my ways," declares the LORD. "As the heavens are higher than the earth, so are my ways higher than your ways and my thoughts than your thoughts."* (Isaiah 55:8-9). Job is about to find out how true this is. God does not appear to Job as his enemy, but as his Creator, who acts for the good of the universe He created. He is not held to account by His creation and Job is invited to reconsider the sheer vastness and incomprehensibility of the created world, and thus, too, the moral order of the universe.

38:4-7

God addresses Job with a series of questions designed to have Job appraise his understanding of creation.

Job has questioned God's moral order and God gives Job no answer to this, rather God begins to question Job about his omniscience, omnipresence and omnipotence in relation to creation. Job, of course, as a work of God's creation cannot speak of creation. Some, in a similar vein to Job's ignorance, might ask, "Why didn't God tell Job why he suffered?" The answer, in part, I believe can be found in Jesus' response to Nicodemus (Jn 3:1ff.). Nicodemus did not understand spiritual issues and struggled to believe them. Jesus says to Nicodemus that if he struggles to comprehend earthly things then there is no way of comprehending heavenly things. There is no way of understanding the reason for Job's suffering, not because there is no reason, and the reader is given some insight from the events in the heavenly council, however that is not the totality of reasons for Job's suffering. Complete understanding is beyond human grasp, hence Peter's admonition to the suffering Christians of the first century (1Pe 4:19). God is taking great pains to help Job understand the depth of wisdom that is needed to comprehend such issues and Job is not slow in picking up on his lack (40:3-5).

38:8-11

Job is asked who set the boundaries of the sea? Inherent in the question is the answer— God. Job was not there to see.

In the ancient Semitic world, control of the boisterous sea was a feature of divine power and authority. The Lord controls the sea by His spoken word (cf. Lk 8:24-25) and 'its doors' are where God set the sea's boundaries. Job cannot possibly have any knowledge of this.

38:12-15

Job has spoken at length about God's dealing with the wicked, now Job is asked if he really understands.

The dawn, too, is beyond Job's comprehension. God is the one who brings morning and it is morning that puts a stop to the acts of the wicked; their morning (that is, their activity begins) is the deep darkness (24:17). The perception is that the earth changes from darkness to morning, in the dawn the earth's features begin to stand out, so too, it is in the 'light' that the deeds of the wicked stand out, and where their power is broken.

38:16-21

God asks Job a series of questions related to his

ability to travel to humanly inaccessible places.

God's control over the unseen world is just as vital as His control over the seen world (cf. 26:5-6). The springs of the sea (v. 16), the recesses (deep trenches) of the sea (v. 16), the gates of death (v. 17), the dwelling of light and darkness (v. 19) are all places from which human beings have been barred. Modern technology has made a little of this accessible, especially the depths of the sea, and yet still so much remains unknown. In God's omnipresence He is in these places, but never Job. Perhaps with a pinch of sarcasm God remarks that Job ought to know these things because he is old (32:6). Elihu has asserted that it is not only the old who are wise (32:9), but Job is not nearly old enough to answer any of God's questions. This round of questioning further reinforces the distance between God's wisdom and man's. Job, who has declared that he has prepared his case can only remain silent.

38:22-30

God continues to question Job about his ability to journey to the inaccessible places and the extent of his understanding of the mysteries of natural phenomena; snow, hail, light, lightning, dew and ice, all of which are beyond Job.

The ancient mind perceived storehouses in which the natural elements were housed and that life was framed within the will of cosmic parents (expressed through the worship of a myriad of gods). Reading with scientific rationalism, this can only be poetry. Science can explain the water cycle, how lightning and thunder is formed as well as the freezing of polar seas during winter. Never in a scientific explanation can there be a personality expressing volition directing natural phenomena. The story of Job is, perhaps, 4000 years old and the people of the earth back then understood the cosmic order differently to Western 21st century thinkers. However, there are people groups today who still consider the cosmos as being spiritually ordered; Buddhists, Hindus and animists to name a few. Many, including Westerners, blend a scientific understanding with a spiritual one, often bound with superstition, and use words like 'karma'. It would seem that an indiscriminate universe is more than unappealing to the majority of human beings. The point that God is making with Job, while not challenging his cosmology, is that natural phenomena functions by design, but not in an automated sense, rather within the purpose of divine will. Nothing escapes God's attention. Jesus alludes to this when he speaks about placing trust in God and considers the worth of a human being compared with that of a sparrow; yet as common as a sparrow might be, it does not die without God's will being enacted over its small life (Mt 10:29; Lk 12:6). If the beauty and sometimes terror of natural phenomena leave us breathless, whether viewed from the perspective of a Yahweh-worshiping ancient near eastern or a God-worshiping 21st century Christian, the message is the same; no matter what your cosmology, behind what is not observable is God enacting His purposeful will, and human beings cannot naturally comprehend it whether they be Job and his companions or the person reading this now. As this series of questions led Job to silence in the presence and majesty of God, so it should for all.

38:31-33

God turns Job's attention to the constellations, asking Job if he can control stars.

Can Job, on earth, determine the laws that govern the constellations?[41] Ancient peoples gave names to the constellations, which are still in use today and no matter what influence they might have on the earth, the people of the earth have no influence on them. God alone orders the stars. Again, Job is brought low—the wisdom and righteousness that he has claimed is insignificant in comparison with God's.

38:34-38

God continues to underscore the limits of Job's stature; implied is Job's (and all creation's) subsequent dependence upon Him.

What can Job do? Can he order the clouds to cover

---

[41] The NIV rendering of 38:33b, "God's dominion over the earth?" could be better translated, 'Can you, on earth, determine the laws that govern them?' See Clines, 'Job', comment, *38:4-38*.

him in mist, send lightning, endow a mind with wisdom (or withhold wisdom), or send water onto a parched land? Job is insignificant compared with God in every way. Job may have been a lord among his people and while holding great sway within his community it cannot compare with the authority to control and maintain the whole of existence.

38:39-41

Job is brought to consider that there is a whole realm of God's creation that is completely independent of man.

Does Job feed the wild animals? These verses lead into the aspect of God's personal concern for nature. Elihu has insisted that God is too remote to engage with His creation intimately, but here Job is given a picture of God's intimate concern for His creation—even to baby ravens—as did Jesus (cf. Mt 6:26ff.; Lk 12:24ff.).

39:1-4

Job is asked about his knowledge of the animal kingdom, particularly in relation to the animals that give birth in the wild; Job had no such awareness as these things, in a sparsely populated land, occurred far from humanity.

God draws Job's attention to the birthing practices of wild creatures, largely unknown at the time and which served no purpose to the human economy.

Mother and newborn are at their most vulnerable at this time and most females give birth hidden from predators. Job, in a world that was not heavily populated, with vast areas of wilderness, had no such knowledge. It is a very different picture today with substantial areas of dense populations, which often drive creatures to extinction, but also much of the natural world is documented and screened on television, and, therefore, many people today have a greater knowledge of the birthing practices of wild creatures. However, the issue is not simply about knowledge; the natural order needs to be sustained and in this part of God's speech He reveals an intimacy and a touch of tenderness toward His creation as He questions Job about these delicate matters, where man was unknowledgeable and gave no assistance.

39:5-8

Job is asked of his knowledge about the freedom that wild donkeys enjoy; does he know why they are untameable?

In the Old Testament the wild donkey was widely admired for its freedom and ability to survive in the harshest of conditions. Completely useless to man, God has exempted it from human service and, thus, also the noise and abuse of animal drivers. There is no way for Job to know how this can be.

39:9-12

Job is questioned about the wild ox; can he

domesticate it?

The wild ox or aurochs[42] (not unicorn, KJV) was used as a symbol of strength (cf. Nu 23:22; 24:8; Dt 33:17; Ps 29:6; et al.), the most powerful of hoofed animals. Here the wild ox is contrasted with the domesticated ox and like the wild donkey it will not submit to human use. The purpose of this creature, along with the wild donkey, is unknown to Job; even today, except for divine pleasure.

39:13-18

When considering the ostrich, God's strength and wisdom are not in view, rather the difficulty in rationalising the natural world, in similar fashion trying to rationalise Job's own suffering—rational answers are often beyond human wisdom.

God speaks of the ostrich—though she was given no wisdom and to human understanding her behaviour of abandoning eggs during the day seems folly, yet God made her fast—only God knows why he has ordained this.

39:19-25

God describes the warhorse's willingness to participate in human warfare, but Job cannot give the

---

[42] The aurochs is extinct and the last recorded aurochs died in the Jaktorów Forest, Poland in 1627. They roamed throughout Eurasia and North Africa.

warhorse its character.

God moves from considering wild animals to domestic; here the horse, specifically the warhorse, and Job is asked if he gives it its strength and flowing mane (v. 19)? Does Job make it fearsome (v. 20) and willing to rush into battle (v. 25)? The warhorse can be harnessed for human use, specifically for battle, but there is no way man can create such a creature.

39:26-30

Job is questioned now about birds of prey; do they live at Job's command?

Job's gaze is directed toward birds; the two cited are generic Hebraic names for several species. Hawk, נֵץ (*nēs*) could be any variety of hawk or falcon; eagle נֶשֶׁר (*nešer*) can be used for eagle or vulture. Some commentators (also NEB) suggest that the bird referred to is the vulture and not the eagle because the griffon vulture is the largest bird of the area and though the same word is used for the eagle (NIV, NRSV, KJV, NASB), here a carrion eater is in mind.[43] It is difficult to be certain; eagles are also known for their soaring, keen eyesight and nesting on high rocky crags, so it is far from certain that vultures are being referred to here. Interestingly, the Septuagint refers to both the eagle (ἀετός) and the vulture (γυψ) in v27, and is probably closer to the original. In any case, Job has no knowledge

---

[43] See Smick, 'Job', comment 39:26-30.

of this either, and like the other animals mentioned, except for the warhorse, they add no value to the human economy, yet they have been given wisdom (v. 26) or natural instincts by God for His pleasure. These creatures exist by the inscrutable will of God, and if Job can accept that, then he can accept the fact that human suffering and the other seeming discrepancies that Job discussed like the prospering of the wicked (21:13), stem, too, from the inscrutable will of God.

40:1-2

Job had requested an audience with God in order to plead his case of unjust suffering, believing that his suffering will then be at an end, and now he is given his opportunity.

Job is given an invitation by Yahweh to respond as he has sought an audience with the Almighty (Shaddai). Was Job now ready, after the survey of God's marvels, to make accusations of His Lordship over the universe?

Suffering cannot simply be an issue of fairness or of injustice on God's part. There must be a deeper truth at work. The parable of the persistent widow (Lk 18:1ff.) indicates that under oppression a person may request justice (or mercy)—but, perhaps, not to accuse God of being unjust; such a statement is not founded in biblical faith. Whatever the antecedent to suffering, God knows and sees all. The just and loving God can release a person from suffering if it serves His purpose. A person can ask God for that—but not charge God with injustice (cf. 6:29).

Job's First Response to God (40:3-5)

40:3-5

As a consequence of God's address, Job has realised the foolishness of his words and knows that now, in his day in court, he has nothing to say.

Job has been cured of his presumption and declares that he is unworthy, which literally means, "I am light", in view of the limitations to his understanding. God has not dealt a crushing blow upon Job, but has helped him to realise that not only is there so much more that can be known, there are also mysteries that belong to God alone, of which Job's suffering is one. Job has tried to put God on trial, but he cannot know how God has put Himself on trial as a result of Satan presumptuously declaring Job's self-centred motive in piety. Throughout the drama Job has not sinned by cursing God, but he is now brought into a greater revelation of God's sovereign majesty. Job's response is to cover his mouth, as if to ensure he speaks no more, for though considered a wise man among his contemporaries, with God in view, he is 'light'.

Yahweh Continues (40:6-41:34)

40:6-14

God is not finished with Job and he is told to brace himself again for further questions about God's majesty from which God will be expecting an answer.

God is still speaking out of the storm (cf. 38:1) and Job's entreaty (vv. 4-5) is not sufficient to assuage God from continuing to have Job perceive himself in a truer light. In Job's last speech he had challenged God (31:35-37), suggesting that any indictment that God might have against him would be false. So much of Job's thinking was imaginative. God had no such indictment against him and Job's understanding had to be corrected for he wrongly assumed that he needed to be vindicated by God. Inherent in God's questions is the idea that Job can only be justified in his complaint if he too has the qualities of the Almighty—if not, his questions, even his justification is out of place. The truth truly makes us lesser beings. Job is challenged to bring just consequences to bear against the wicked. Wickedness, and how and when God deals with the wicked, has been at the heart of Eliphaz, Bildad, Zophar and Elihu's response to Job's suffering. Now Job is challenged to unleash the fury of his wrath and look at every proud man and bring him to nothing. God concedes that if Job can act with divine authority then he has the inherent power to save himself, that is, be vindicated. However, both God and Job know that Job can do none of this. Job has challenged the moral order of the universe and placed himself at its centre, as so many have since. The natural consequence is a condemnation of God and the exaltation of the person.

Job, like most human beings, can talk of how things ought to be and describe what is wrong with the world. However, what he might be able to alter according to the good he could do is insufficient to affect the moral order of the universe. To do good is right, to make permanent universal change is impossible. God reveals to Job that the man cannot save himself, let alone others.

40:15-24

Job is asked to consider the behemoth, which has strength and size unrivalled, too powerful for trapping or taming, but which God can approach without fear.

Along with man, God made creatures hostile and resistant to man, which cannot be captured or dominated. Therefore, it is wise for humans to leave them well alone, yet God can approach such colossal creatures with ease. The thrust of the text is that this creature, though unsubmissive to man, will willingly submit to its creator. This image continues the theme of God's sovereign majesty over the universe compared with Job. The behemoth is the plural of בְּהֵמוֹת (bᵉhemah), 'land creature', mostly translated as 'animal' or 'livestock'. The behemoth בְּהֵמוֹת (bᵉhemôt) *can be translated as* 'the great beast'.[44] It has been variously

---

44 See Clines, *Job*, comment, 40:15-24.

described as a hippopotamus, elephant, wild buffalo, a sauropod or a mythical creature. Along with the leviathan, the force of the text suggests that these are real creatures created by God, and known to Job. Myth has certainly surrounded these creatures due to their size and ferocity, especially of the leviathan, and they are symbolic of primeval chaos and God's control of the chaotic powers that might threaten the universe. However, this does not mean that they were not real creatures.

A known creature that best fits the description of the behemoth is the hippopotamus. However, the description of its tail that sways like a cedar (v. 17) cannot possibly fit, and the metaphor of his bones being tubes of bronze (v. 18), in this case, would seem too hyperbolic and, therefore, inconsistent with the rest of the description. There is no need, I believe, to assign an identity to the behemoth, nor to identify it with mythopoeic language. If we are to read the book of Job as a retelling of an actual event, as opposed to highly symbolic wisdom literature, and believe that this is indeed the voice of God from the thunderstorm speaking to Job, it would seem unlikely that God is in the process of composing a myth or speaking of the product of myth as if it were real. Many creatures have become extinct over the last five thousand years or so (many would say over a much longer period), some more recently extinct, for example the Dusky Seaside

Sparrow,[45] were well known, others are only known from fossils, and perhaps there is a myriad of creatures never to be known. Many commentators suggest that the behemoth, first among God's creatures (v. 19), possibly an allusion to Genesis 1:21, where the great creatures of the sea are mentioned, is best identified with the hippopotamus, however, I would suggest it is best to read it as it is described and accept that it was a real creature, which has vanished along with any clear knowledge of it apart from God's word.

41:1-11

As the Supreme Being, God alone has the power to subdue the leviathan, therefore this is an example that He is answerable to no one and, thus, Job has no claim to put before Him.

The leviathan is a creature that, like the other creatures mentioned (38:39-39:30), except the warhorse, is of no value, certainly of no commercial value to human beings. Not only is it untameable like the behemoth, it is also ferocious. If God can rouse him without fear, then no man can stand against God. If the creatures of the earth are beyond Job's understanding and the great creatures beyond his power, Job is far removed from the sovereign majesty of the God who contains them all. Job, who said that he would give free reign to his complaint and speak out of the bitterness of

---

[45] The Dusky Seaside Sparrow was found in Florida, USA. The last known individual died in 1987.

his soul (10:1) and argue his case (13:3), is given no right at all.

Many commentators suggest that the description given of the leviathan depicts a mythological image of the crocodile, but there is no need to force the text to denote a known creature in order to satisfy modern readers. Just as God pointed out to Job that there is much within the universe that is beyond his knowing, some of what he does know is incomprehensible and some terrifying; the same is true of modern humanity, even with the advances in technology. Job is learning that there is much mystery in the universe and for the modern reader of Job, that has not changed. Mythology does surround the leviathan and it is mentioned in ancient texts other than the Old Testament. It is also mentioned in Psalm 104:6, Job 3:8 and Isaiah 27:1 in which a creature far more terrifying than a crocodile appears to be in mind. Perhaps it is best to accept the leviathan as a mysterious creature that once existed, but today cannot be identified.

41:12-34

God describes to Job the fearlessness of the leviathan. It has no equal and is terrifying and mysterious, but still part of God's world, with splendour and purpose known only to God and that is the same place where Job's suffering is to be found.

After the climax of God's speech (vv. 10-11) comes a detailed description of a creature far beyond the characteristics of a crocodile. God is illustrating His point, using the leviathan and behemoth that He made earlier (40:8-14); that Job has no arm like His, no glory nor splendour; One who triumphs morally over evil as He has done through Job over Satan. Job is challenged to think of the most powerful, enigmatic and frightening creature and see it as God's pet, submissive to His will. Contained within the universe are features beyond his knowing, but are in the direct control of God; so too Job's suffering and he must suffer in ignorance.

Job's Second Response to God (42:1-6)

42:1-6

Job answers God by acknowledging that it is God's purpose that counts and, though still suffering, he has been comforted by the presence of His God.

Job's final speech is evidence of his resolution with God. His complaint has been that his suffering made no sense—it was against the generally subscribed theological rules of guilt and punishment. God has brought Job to a place of understanding that God is right to do what He does, without question. Though it is not made explicit, it is implied that God is even right in bringing suffering to an innocent person because, as Job's suffering might not make sense to him, it does to God and ultimately that is what matters. It is enough for Job to know that God knows what He is doing.

Job is, at this point, still suffering, still on the ash pile, but what his friends could not do, neither by their presence nor speeches, which Job had wished they would do (16:1-5), God has now done. Job has now found peace and comfort in the purposes of God even though those purposes are much less than he would desire and completely enigmatic. As Job has now seen and heard God, he finds that he cannot give an answer to God's questions, the case he prepared has collapsed. In the Hebrew 'myself' [KJV, NIV, NRSV; NASB is better] (v. 6) does not appear and it would seem certain that it is the words without knowledge that he has hurled toward God that he despises, though it is possible that Job may not differentiate between the two, that is, himself and his words. The Septuagint translates 'despise' as 'melt' as David Clines helpfully describes v. 6a, 'I melt into nothingness', the feeling of a creature before his creator."[46] Job is brought low, but not in the sense of being abased, but to see himself in the clearer light of his Creator.

Job repents. He certainly will not speak in such a way again, however, the word repent נָחַם *(nāham)* also has the meaning to comfort. Thus, through this encounter with God, Job has seen afresh his God's sovereign majesty. He has understood that there was much he did not comprehend nor could comprehend and though still suffering, he has been comforted—Job can trust his God. The faith that he had in God prior to this great calamity, while shaken to its core, has been

---

[46] See Clines, *Job,* comment 42:1-6.

revitalised and, arguably, placed on a better foundation.

Job has not asked God to take his suffering away, only for an explanation as to why he, an innocent man, should be suffering. An answer to Job's question is never given and God has made it clear that no answer would be forthcoming. Rather, God has purposes beyond human comprehension and the person of faith needs to trust that God knows and is working out His purposes, which His whole creation is incapable of avoiding. Had God answered Job's question it would render impotent the comfort his story offers for those who suffer without seeming cause. Though Job is not given an explanation, the reader is given partial understanding. Job, in part, has suffered as God's vindication of him against Satan's accusation and thus Job's suffering is not to humiliate him, but instead, the Accuser.

42:7

God declares that Eliphaz, Bildad and Zophar have not spoken the truth.

God is angry with Job's friends because of the way they have portrayed Him. Job, himself, has said things of God that were inaccurate as well. Job has asked why God considered him an enemy (13:24) and his last words (31:35-37) questioned God's integrity, suggesting that any accusation brought by God against Job would prove to be false. This was, of course, hypothetical nonsense and came from Job's imagination. God has made no accusations against Job, rather He has commended Job. Job believed that he needed vindication by God, but that was never the case. However, it is his friends that God said have spoken wrongly about Him, not Job. Job has said God was attacking him (30:21) and the friends all agreed. Job questioned God's motives and asked, "Why, for I am an innocent man?" His friends did not concur, instead they all believed that Job was a guilty man and deserved punishment. Not that they had any evidence of Job's wrongdoing, their conclusions were drawn from Job's circumstances; guilt by association. Eliphaz, in particular, had heard the hushed voice of a spirit (4:15ff.) which formed the basis of his arguments about Job and thus God's dealings with Job, but these were clearly not from the Spirit of God. The friends could not have been more wrong about God's motivations toward Job.

It ought to be remembered and reflected upon with some sobriety that all Job's friends sought to uphold and defend God. One of the subtle differences between Job and his friends is that they all talked about God in an objective and distant manner. Job, too, talked about God, but so much of his dialogue was, in actual fact, addressed to God. It is all too easy to hold theological ideas, true or otherwise, about God without ever engaging with God personally. Job's friends' theological position held a God too transcendent for personal interaction. Job, however, portrays through his speeches, prior to his suffering, a level of intimacy with God and this is confirmed as God speaks to

Ezekiel (14:14, 20). Jesus said to His disciples that a time was coming when anyone who killed them would think that he was offering a service to God (Jn 16:2) and explained that such behaviour comes from religious people who do not know the Father or Himself. There is no substitute for a relationship with the Father through faith in the Son; it is the cornerstone for life, truth and love. Those who would defend God without ever really knowing Him cannot act like nor speak for God for His Spirit is not in them; they cannot but incur His wrath, as Job's friends had (cf. Jn 5:36ff.). However, even though God was angry with Eliphaz, Bildad and Zophar He showed them His loving kindness. They had said that Job was getting what he deserved from God, though in a wonderful, graceful glorious, twist, God did not give them what they deserved; He is merciful!

42:8-9

God speaks to Eliphaz and requires him and Bildad and Zophar to present burnt offerings for the wrong things they have spoken about Him and for the now vindicated Job to act as their priest.

The friends who have felt superior to Job are now, by divine decree (v. 8), in need of him. Four times God calls Job His servant, which is Job's vindication and perhaps this helps Job to appreciate that his suffering was not due in any way to God's anger toward him, though, in this life at least, he will never know the reasons behind it. The large sacrifice indicates the seriousness with which God viewed their whole approach toward Job. They had not appreciated the heavenly drama and spoke from their own perceptions founded on the words of a spirit (4:15) and conventional wisdom (8:8; 20:4), judging Job as a sinner receiving due punishment. God labels their response to Job and their subsequent misrepresentation of Him as נְבָלָה (*nᵉbēlâ*) very wicked (NIV folly), which denotes a wicked person rather than merely a person who lacks sense and is often translated 'disgraceful thing' (cf. Ge 34:7; Dt 22:21; Jos 7:15; Jdg 19:23-24). However, instead of receiving what was due, God offered them repentance in the form of presenting offerings, and forgiveness through His acceptance of Job's prayer for them. Their theology had maintained that God rightly punishes sinners and Job was receiving what he deserved. In a wonderful twist and with an opportunity for them to reappraise their theology rather than receive what their theology determined they ought, they accepted God's offer of forgiveness and went to Job.

Job's Restoration (42:10-17)

42:10-11

God restores Job's fortunes and now he receives the comfort from his family that he had hoped to receive during his suffering.

Job has been restored in the eyes of his friends, but

naturally for this restoration to be understood by his community, they need to see him prosperous again. Job's friends have undergone a transformation in their thinking, but not so for Job's community. They would still hold to a rigid doctrine of retribution and were unlikely to appreciate God's favour upon Job without the commensurate prosperity, thus God exalts Job in their eyes through a double measure of material blessing. Upon the restoration of Job's fortunes, his family and community come and comfort him. There is no doubt as to the source of Job's suffering, but now that he has been restored they feel that they need not keep their distance from him. Along with words of comfort they each bring him a gift of silver and a gold ring, thus further adding to his wealth. These gifts are not given to alleviate his poverty, but more as a sign of their contrition in relation to their wrongful judgement upon him.

42:12-15

Job receives greater blessing, gaining more wealth and receiving children again.

The increase of Job's possessions is twofold (cf. 1:3) except for his children; he remains with seven sons and three daughters (cf. 1:2). Unusually, it is the daughters who are mentioned in detail and they receive an inheritance along with their brothers. Beautiful women have been and remain highly esteemed in most cultures and Job's daughters are described as the most beautiful in theirs. Their names are an indication of their beauty.

The first-born daughter, Jemimah, means little dove. Herbert Lockyer points out that the Septuagint renders Jemimah as originating from the Hebrew word for day, so her name could mean 'bright or beautiful as day.'[47] Job's second daughter, Keziah, is the feminine noun for the fragrance of the cassia flower. Job's third daughter, Keren-Happuch, is called horn of (eye) paint. Her name speaks of a vessel containing cosmetics, frequently made from horn.[48] Her name is indicative of beautiful eyes enhanced by cosmetics that make them more lustrous (cf. 2Ki 9:30; Jer 4:30).

42:16-17

Job's story finishes with an image of serene blessing; he is full of years surrounded by his family to the fourth generation and dies a complete man.

The epilogue brings to a close the drama in a way that is typical of the patriarchal narratives of Genesis with death following a life 'full of years'. Job's age is unknown at the beginning of the drama; certainly old enough to have grown children. After his suffering it is as if Job's life is born again and he lives a further 140 years. This is the final blessing of God (cf. Ge 25:8; 35:29). The final scene evokes the sense of the idyllic mood in which the story began. However, the tranquil

---

[47] Herbert Lockyer, 'Jemima', *All The Women in the Bible on CD-ROM*, (Grand Rapids: Zondervan, nd.).
[48] Herbert Lockyer, 'Keren-Haapuch', *All The Women in the Bible on CD-ROM*, (Grand Rapids: Zondervan, nd.).

ending belies the fact that there has been a drama of great suffering of a type that can be observed in every age. Throughout the drama Job held onto his integrity and proved, whether in prosperity or poverty, that he would worship God, and thus this old story is a paradigm for how a successful life is to be lived today; "The fear of the Lord—that is wisdom, and to shun evil is understanding." (28:28).

THE BEHEMOTH AND THE LEVIATHAN

Towards the end of the book when God speaks to Job, He speaks of His sovereign majesty over the earth. The order of the universe is recounted; things that Job knows little about. God mentions specific wild animals which have no value to the human economy and at the time of the setting of the story little is known about these creatures. Specifically named are lions, ravens, wild goats, deer, wild donkey, wild ox (aurochs), ostrich, warhorse, hawk, eagle and vulture (see Septuagint). While Job knows little of the zoology of these animals, he is aware of their existence, and so to, for the most part the modern reader. God then speaks in more detail of two creatures of which now nothing is conclusively known—the behemoth and the leviathan. The inclusion of these two creatures has been the catalyst for much contention and even for a wholesale dismissal of the whole Book of Job as being God's word by some because they are unidentifiable— perhaps the whole story of Job is just then mythology—a dramatic, though fictional story told to make a point. Especially so since the leviathan is not only metaphorically referenced elsewhere in the Old Testament (Ps 7414; 104:26; Isa 27:1) but also in

Canaanite literature.[49]

The truth is there is no way of identifying these creatures with any certainty (even radiocarbon dating is said to only reliably date to 50,000 years ago), however, that is not reason to quickly dismiss them and the example they serve for Job's understanding. The reason for their inclusion is clear—God's sovereign power over all that He has made and that God delights in the things that human beings find mysterious and even terrifying. For the sake of the integrity of the Book of Job these creatures ought to be taken seriously and our assumptions with regard to their identity have serious theological implications. Is it reasonable to accept that such creatures actually existed alongside human beings so that Job understood exactly what God was telling him with regard to them?

The behemoth and leviathan have been variously described as mythological creatures, dinosaurs, elephants, the hippopotamus, wild ox (aurochs), the crocodile or whale. Perhaps many readers glance over the names behemoth and leviathan and give them and their descriptions little attention and settle for the thrust of the text being God's sovereignty even over the most awesome and fearsome of creatures. The question might arise, does it matter if these creatures

---

[49] Lita Cosner. (Dec, 2013). Leviathan—real or symbolic? *Creation.com.* https://creation.com/leviathan-real-or-symbolic Mart-Jan Paul. (Dec, 2010). Behemoth and leviathan in the book of Job. *Creation.Com.* https://creation.com/behemoth-and-leviathan

can be positively identified or not? And perhaps at a superficial level it doesn't, after all the behemoth and leviathan are at this point in history unidentifiable, as is so much of human history, let alone natural history. However, glossing over these creatures as undefinable and labelling them 'most probably'—the behemoth as a hippopotamus or elephant, and the leviathan as a crocodile, even a larger version of the Nile crocodile, or whale as many commentators and notes in study Bibles do, not only does not do the story justice, it has implications regarding how we might read the rest of the Bible. It raises questions about beliefs about God, cosmology and the truth of the Bible.

Modern palaeontology sheds no light on these creatures, and perhaps it would be considered in its best interests not to link them, as they potentially could affect the well-established evolutionary timeline. While the evolutionary timeline is commonly accepted as an established scientific inviolable fact, in reality it cannot be so absolute, simply because there is no possible means of verification. Like it or not, the whole theory of evolution can be no more than science's best guess, using selected evidence to piece together the puzzle of our origin, and arguably an origin that suits a non-theistic worldview. In other words in order to understand these creatures a little better, while not ignoring the evidence unearthed of the earth's forgotten past, there is more to be gained by looking at the internal consistency of the story itself rather than dismissing, fabricating or using ill-fitting transformations.

How do we read the story of Job?

The story of Job can be read, as with any story, from different perspectives. It can be read as a piece of ancient semi-fictitious literature as in Homer's Iliad and Odyssey; a Hebraic Wisdom text used to symbolise the sovereignty of Yahweh—full of mythology; or an allegorical story with the writer's imagined dialogue between the characters conveying God's cosmic sovereignty. Another view is that the story is simply a retelling of events as they occurred. Despite many churches making a statement of faith regarding the inerrancy and/or trustworthiness of the Bible as God's word, the people of those church's confidence in it quickly breaks down when the magnifying glass is enlarging this and other difficult issues. And so the reader can happily assign these creatures to the same place where the census lists of Numbers and Chronicles, the items for the tabernacle and which tribe sacrificed what and so forth is assigned, largely irrelevant and forgotten, if read at all. It is unlikely that the typical Christian reading Job would have the 'hermeneutical spiral'[50] in mind in order to consider its deeper complexities, however, the viewpoint from which a person reads determines the

---

[50] Grant Osborne coined the term 'hermeneutical spiral' and it means that biblical interpretation entails a spiral from the text being read to the context in which it is written, from the original meaning to its significance or meaning for the church today. Grant R. Osborne, *The Hermeneutical Spiral*, (Downers Grove, Illinois: IVP, 2006).

message in general, and specifically here, how the behemoth and leviathan ought to be viewed. In all perspectives mentioned, except the latter, these two creatures can be relegated to mythology if that seems desirable, or as a hyperbolic description of known animals such as the hippopotamus or crocodile. However, using mythology or hyperbole to describe these creatures is inconsistent with the rest of the text. If the perspective is taken that the book of Job belongs to the canon because it is part of the infallible word of God in an orthodox evangelical sense, that the book of Job is not simply written in mythopoeic language, but is history that God would have revealed, then, because of the context in which these creatures are placed, that is alongside other known creatures and astrological bodies, then it becomes dismissive to assign them to mythology or even to a species of dinosaur that became extinct long before human beings ever walked the earth, or even to refer to them as a hippopotamus or crocodile using ill-fitting descriptions. If Job is to be read as the inerrant word of God there needs to be a better explanation than is found in many commentaries, study Bibles and Bible dictionaries.

Long earth or short earth?

With a bit of creative theologising the behemoth and the leviathan can be consigned to the dinosaur age using a long/old earth theory. Long earth creationists,[51] specifically theistic evolutionists, are typically inclined to a view of creation that is compatible with mainstream scientific thought and accept an evolutionary time scale of millions of years, in which, for instance, dinosaurs were well extinct before the advent of homo sapiens—a gap of about 60 million years. With this view in mind the behemoth and leviathan could not be descriptions of species of dinosaur as they would have been completely unknown to Job—God questions Job about things of which he has some experience. If a person's presupposition when approaching the Bible, and particularly the creation account, is a long earth theistic evolutionist timeline, then to describe these creatures as dinosaurs (a sauropod, pholidosaurs, even a theropod[52]) is problematic. In order to do so, such a person must ignore God's clear assumption that Job understands perfectly the animals He is describing

---

[51] Long or Old Earth Creationism is an umbrella term for a number of types of creationism, including gap creationism, progressive creationism, evolutionary creationism, and Hindu creationism.

[52] Sauropods had very long necks, long tails, small heads, and four thick, pillar-like legs, e.g. the brontosaurus.

Pholidosaurs are giant crocodilian creatures, the best known being the sarcosuchus.

Theropods are characterized by hollow bones and three-toed limbs; thought originally to be carnivores, the tyrannosaurus rex is a well-known example.

Perhaps it should be noted that classifications and descriptions of dinosaur type creatures change regularly because little is conclusively known about them.

along with the animals still known today—even the aurochs (39:9) which is now extinct. As a result of the difficulty of using an evolutionary timeline to describe these creatures as types of dinosaurs, most do not bother to try and therefore, must consign the descriptions to known animals.

Short earth creationists who accept the Genesis six days of creation (Ge 1:1-31) cannot accept an evolutionary timeline as theistic evolutionists do. Not all, though, accept a literal six 24 hour days of creation and will often cite a thousand years being like a day and vice versa (Ps 90:4; 2Pe 3:8), and will concede to six periods which they will equate to days, though in the context of the creation account the use of the word יוֹם (*yôm*) day coupled with an ordinal number (first, second, third etc.) indicates a 24-hour period (so also the Septuagint [ημέρα; day]). The six days become six periods, though not considered in millions of years, perhaps six periods of a thousand years each. This is the convenient middle ground 'out' some want due to the weight of worldwide consensus that argues for a world much older than a possible six thousand years founded on the Hebrew genealogies beginning with Adam.

There is no good exegetical reason for doing so with the text of Genesis chapter one because the words do not allow for it. However, Genesis chapter two defies that argument if it is read under the assumption that the same author (presumably Moses) wrote it as the natural follow-on from the general creation account to a more detailed account of the creation of man—man being the focus of creation. In chapter one we are told that man and woman were created on the sixth day (Ge 1:26, 31). In chapter two we are told that man was created first and placed in the garden of Eden. There he worked the garden and was given instruction regarding the fruit of the tree of the knowledge of good and evil. He also named the animals and at this point God said that it was not good for man to be alone and consequently created woman out of man. These events, then, surely took longer than one 24-hour period, but in terms of Genesis chapter one, all occurred on the sixth day.

So, where does that leave us? A literal reading of the creation account only allows for six 24-hour periods, and the events of chapter two would have taken longer than one literal days' worth of events on day six. The assumption that I would make is that the word 'day' in Genesis chapter one along with its ordinal number, while literally meaning a 24-hour period, is used theologically and not phenomenologically. God can and does call something morning and evening without the sun and the moon being created (the first three days)—we cannot limit God to human experience and reason. Thus the word יוֹם *(yôm)* day with an ordinal following, while literally meaning a 24 hour period, is being used theologically and thus does not limit those specific days to 24-hour periods as the word 'day' is being used descriptively not prescriptively—Genesis chapter two indicates that they were not. There is one instance in the Old Testament when a day lasted longer than a 24-hour period; Joshua's defeat of the Amorites (Jos 10:5-14). It is also possible that Hezekiah's sign of the shadow going backwards on the step also meant a longer day (2Ki 20:11; 2Chr 32:31).

In saying that, there is no indication at all as to how long those creation days could have been or even if they were consistent periods—there would be no necessity for it. However, short earth creationists, no matter what their position on the six-day timeframe, agree that the earth is not as old as the evolutionary time scale supposes and, perhaps more importantly, that creatures which were extinct according to evolutionary thinking were not extinct at all but shared the earth with mankind for some time. Non-European and Near Eastern cultures have dinosaurs in their folklore. The modern argument reasons that the folklore is based on the fossils and bones that they knew of because they could not have known the animals. However, while people groups did know of bones and fossils that does not presuppose that that is the only reason for there being folklore.

If the reader accepts that the story of Job is a retelling of actual events, then God is speaking (Chs. 38-41), and not the writer proposing what God might say. The descriptions He gives of the behemoth and leviathan must then be accurate because God does not lie and Job would understand what they are, in similar fashion to understanding what a hawk or wild donkey is, because understanding is implied in the address. This would indicate that they are not merely mythological creatures.[53] Long earth theory, from a theistic viewpoint, cannot accept these creatures being dinosaurs (a sauropod or a sarcosuchus [a theropod being a land animal is less likely]) and must consign them to known creatures even though the descriptions do not match. A short earth theory can accept the possibility of these creatures being a type of dinosaur without being dogmatic on their exact identity. In this case, clearly, a long earth theory has blinkers on and thus violates the message of the story at this point.

Where is the evidence?

It would seem at this point that palaeontologists have not been prepared to link any remains (fossils, bones or imprints) discovered to these creatures though there might be a resemblance from the descriptions in 40:15-34—of course doing so would not serve their interests. The creature, leviathan, is described in stories of the Ancient Near East,[54] often representing a monster of chaos, however, ancient stories alone are not proof enough. With no certain proof, readers are consigned to opinions based on their beliefs about the Bible and their scientific worldview which are often held in

---

[53] That is not to say that mythology did not surround them, especially as so many creatures were and are deified by ancient and not so ancient peoples. Even the accounts associated with the Israelite Patriarchs reveal some superstitious thinking.

[54] See Maarten J. Paul's article, 'Leviathan', *New International Dictionary of Old Testament Theology and Exegesis on CD-ROM*, (Grand Rapids: Zondervan, n.d.).

contradiction.

Lack of existing demonstrable proof of coexistence with man does not in itself mean that these creatures, if not the hippopotamus and crocodile, did not exist during the lifetime of Job. Absence of proof proves nothing. Many species have become extinct, especially in times more recent than the Old Testament, and little is known about them. The thylacine (Tasmanian tiger) is a case in point; as a result of intensive hunting it has become extinct (circa 1936) and today, despite how recent its demise, little is known about it. Only a few rare photos exist. Even less is known of the thylacine as it lived on the Australian mainland long before British colonization. Without its existence on Tasmania it is possible that the thylacine would have remained unknown. The indigenous peoples did not carry its memory in their oral folklores. As such a lack of evidence isn't enough to presuppose non-existence or non-coexistence. The giant flightless bird of New Zealand, the moa, is only known today because of the various bones that have been found, mainly from drained swamps after European settlers drained them for farming, and in some caves. It is believed that the early colonisers of the country, the Maori, predated upon them through to extinction approximately three hundred years prior to European settlement. Pre-European Maori culture, being oral, passed their history through story and as the moa had disappeared so too, over successive generations, did its story as it was no longer relevant to life in their present.[55] Not until Europeans started draining swamps for farmland, with the discovery of large bird bones, did any readily existent knowledge about these birds materialize, and that was in no way substantial, rather a vague recounting. The moa and up to half of New Zealand's bird species were extinct by 1770. The knowledge of them is gained through modern archaeological investigation. Clearly, with both the thylacine and the moa, an absence of common knowledge does not prove that a creature never existed. Perhaps a time will come when more might be known about these and other creatures that have disappeared.

It is not just oral cultures that fixate on the now. Even with biblical studies interpretation focuses on the present, as if the present was the sum of all that has been, and that can lead to significant error. After the destruction of the nation of Israel by the Romans (circa 70 AD), despite the prophetic indications of the existence of a literal nation of Israel being in existence at the end of the age, because of Israel's non-existence, the notion appeared fanciful to many biblical scholars before the twentieth century. Yet since 1948 the nation of Israel is a literal fact and despite the chagrin of the nations around them and their attempts to destroy Israel, the nation exists and thrives, arguably the most prosperous nation in the Middle East. God spoke of

---

[55] See Michael King's account of Maori settlement, The Penguin History of New Zealand, (Auckland: Penguin, 2003), 15-75.

Israel's existence through His prophets, so it shall be. Granted the nation of Israel did not exist for almost 2000 years. However, interpreting God's word for the present, without the prophetic eye for what is still to come, led to mythologising God's word and built a section of the church full of unbelief that exists to this day. If, as in Job's case regarding the leviathan and the behemoth, God has spoken it, so it must be as it has been described with those descriptions being completely inconsistent with a hippopotamus or crocodile. Just as God spoke of the nation of Israel being in existence at the time of Christ's return.

The story of Job is wrapped in the inexorably inscrutable will of God. While the reader can understand that there is a spiritual dynamic to the story, of which the central human characters are unaware, the reader though is not privy to the reasons why God allowed his favoured servant to suffer in the way He did. Job's suffering ultimately remains a mystery to us as does so much of God's purpose within the universe He created. Therefore, to simply consign the behemoth and the leviathan to mythology or highly hyperbolic descriptions of known animals because of a lack of proof is entirely unnecessary.

Trust in God's word

Acceptance of God's word as being true and reliable means that within the framework of the contexts of the books, their genre, intended audience, milieu and so forth, we ought to accept as truth the things we might not yet understand—letting the text dictate. Organised religion believes it has a great soul and equally great intellectual prowess (despite what the atheist might think), along with an unmatched hold on God, as if God were shackled within their inner sanctum. Trust in God's word, particularly in terms of a straightforward reading, is usually not encouraged by the ecclesiastical elite. A distrust of God's word was significantly fuelled by the development of Higher German criticism (late C18) within the reformed tradition of Western Christendom, of which Protestant liberalism was an early fruit (which has matured and produced Christianised religious tares of many kinds). The tree of distrust of God's word continues to bear fruit fuelled by all manner of violation leaving many believers confused, wavering in their faith, and distrusting. However, while some things might be hard to understand and some explanation is helpful, for the most part a straightforward reading of the Bible gives a Christian all that God wants His children to know through it and is easy to grasp. Accepting that is still a matter of faith. Therefore, as the behemoth and leviathan are described to Job in the same fashion as the other animals described, that is, Job has knowledge of them, they ought to be read as known to Job as described, even though for the modern reader their exact identity is a mystery; just as Job knew of the animals described, but so much about them was a mystery to him. There is no reason to suggest that it is any different with these two mysterious creatures. They ought to be accepted as the story suggests, as described by God (through the author): one, a mighty herbivore, perhaps a sauropod dinosaur, and the other a powerful and dangerous dragon-like, creature, perhaps a sarcosuchus, or something even more terrifying. Their exact identity may forever be lost to antiquity, but they were presented as real, awesome, even terrifying and beyond the control of man, thus untameable, even deified, but living under the direct control of God as is all life. Therefore, the behemoth and the leviathan should be accepted as such, as written, and no attempt ought to be made to go beyond the word of God, or even with good intentions try to repair in order to fit the present, as the present is not the sum of all that has been—that is God's position.

ELIPHAZ, BILDAD AND ZOPHAR — A MODEL FOR FALSE PROPHETS AND TEACHERS WHO WOULD FOLLOW

As Job sat in the ash heap contemplating his misery, three friends, men of no small means themselves, visited him to bring comfort. Over the years they have been facetiously labelled as Job's Comforters. It is a sarcastic epithet because they did not comfort Job at all and at the conclusion of the story God Himself is angry with what they have said. However, despite them failing in their attempt to help Job and bring him into God's blessing it would appear that their motives were honourable. Perhaps then a certain level of sympathy may be extended to them because they meant well. As with much well-meant advice they ended their counsel in frustration as a result of Job's refusal to heed their guidance and all came to the same conclusion that Job was a hopeless case—including Elihu who joined them later. They concluded that Job was suffering from self-delusion and in so many ways the worst of sinners—righteous in his own eyes (32:1). The friends' approach to their counsel was theological. Job's suffering was from God, to which Job agreed, but the cause of suffering being Job's sin, with that Job would not agree. Their attempted counsel was to bring Job to repentance before God in order for God to relent of the punishment that He had, in their understanding, so rightly dispensed. In the process of trying to persuade Job to accept their reason much was said about God, and Eliphaz, Bildad, Zophar and Elihu took it upon themselves to be God's spokesperson. This was not explicitly said, but implicit in their words and actions they each became Job's prophet, teacher and counsellor. If their attempts to help Job were truly well-meant and even though they could not convince Job, then we, the modern reader being people of our zeitgeist might be inclined to cheer them on and at least thank them for trying—after all, they went to help. We might even consider God to have been a little hard in His anger toward Eliphaz, Bildad and Zophar, who amid all the dialogues spoke clearly about God and sought to uphold His honour. Yet God was not pleased and of the five human characters in this drama, three were singled out as having spoken wrongly of Him and only Job is vindicated as speaking rightly of God (42:7). The information upon which they would build a case against Job came from conventional wisdom, which had a clear theological cause and effect thinking—man sins, God punishes. However, overlaid on that worldview was a word given by a spiritual source. This then gave them an authority beyond the merely natural, hence their utter frustration when he would not heed their advice—it wasn't just them, in their thinking, Job was rejecting. If we were to leap many centuries into the 21st, and look within the contemporary church we can witness many people who reprise the role of Eliphaz, Bildad and Zophar: people speaking claiming a spiritual source; people who give theological counsel, who are, by and large, well-intentioned, who want to see others brought to God; people claiming to be God's spokesperson, who expect a hearing and a following (of their advice at the very least), though not all get it. The role of Job's friends is reprised in that they give theological counsel, usually with direct reference to a spiritual source (overlaid upon their prevailing worldview) and arguably continue to speak wrongly of God. The church in its current milieu makes little attempt to curtail the situation, and many Christians rather than reprise the role of Job, happily go along with what is said in the name of God in the hope of receiving the many blessings they are told that God has on offer. If the story of Job is old, occurring at the time of Israel's Patriarch's then that would make Eliphaz, Bildad and Zophar the first recorded false prophets/teachers of the Bible and in many ways a template for the many false prophets that Jesus said would appear towards the end of the age (Mt 24:11, 24; Mk 13:22; Lk 21:8).

Being well intentioned is not enough

Job's friends came with the purpose of help—from God's perspective good intentions then are not enough. Perhaps this is the most insidious aspect of the false prophets of our current era, for the most part they are well-intentioned. There may be some people who have evil intent with a desire to purposely mislead, but they would appear to be the minority. Most have benevolent intentions, and this is why it is the most insidious. Encouragement is a significant Western value. In school sports, particularly in primary (elementary) schools, participation is esteemed over winning so that those who do not win do not have their self-esteem damaged. Teachers in many cases are not even to put a red cross by a wrong answer using the same reasoning. In the church fire and brimstone preaching has given way to encouragement, and corrective prophetic words must be avoided in order for people to be encouraged, meaning feel good about themselves and thus keep coming to church. This has given rise to the ethos of sentimentality, which fuels claims of God's and heaven's overwhelmingly intense emotional (in human terms) concern for every individual expressed in language inconsistent within the biblical narrative.

We live in an age where sentiment often passes for faith for the regular churchgoer and concomitant with that is the importance of feelings of tenderness, happiness, sadness and nostalgia expressed in the contemporary worship of God within the context of a worship service. When sentiment passes as faith, we open the door for all manner of permissiveness into the church, with church leaders having little in the way of authority to address it if they have a mind to. With specific regard to the Pentecostal, Charismatic and Dominionist movements, one of the explosions has been the rise of untested prophetic pronouncements. The prophetic voice is heard in small groups, in local churches, self-styled prophetic ministries, large and small, also voiced by the leaders of mega-churches with television ministries. It would be difficult to find many who have purposeful evil motive in that their intended reason for uttering forth 'a word', claiming it is from God, is to lead people into sin or away from God—the opposite they would claim. Like Eliphaz, Bildad and Zophar before them they truly want to help in accordance with their prescribed theological assumptions. They see a world in need of accepting God's salvation and once accepted they want to help people to enter into all the blessing that they, according to their theology, believe followers of Christ are entitled. I am not suggesting this is the only motive, but that is something with which most on the evangelical spectrum would agree. However, when sentiment drives much of the world, and that spirit is in the church, even if the prophets are wrong in what they say, because they present as being well-intentioned, sentiment washes over what is false without a care because truth is not the cornerstone of the prophetic anymore.

Prophecies must come from God and therefore be true

In part the church's, as in the broad spectrum of Bible believing evangelicals, confidence in the Scriptures is based on the belief that the Old Testament prophecies will come to pass and particularly that the prophets, Isaiah through to Malachi, accurately spoke the truth as God's Spirit inspired them; their proclamations are accepted as being entirely true. The prophets were speaking/writing as guided by the Holy Spirit (Zec 7:12; 2Pe 1:21), thus they were not speaking simply conventional wisdom, nor from their own concerns, but rather as mouthpieces for God. Today none of the biggest names in the Pentecostal, Charismatic and Dominionist movements claim 100% accuracy (I could give many names and examples, but have chosen not to, as an easy internet search would reveal who they are and the false claims made), and this does not seem to raise much in the way of alarm bells. Prophecies regarding revivals, earthquakes, tsunamis, financial uplift, the end of the 2020 coronavirus pandemic with dates that come and go do not seem to impact negatively on the so-called prophet's ministry, rather in a strange twist of human justification, the prophets are held onto with entrenched vigour.

None of this is new. Perhaps what is new is the explosion of false prophets/teachers and gullible Christians hanging onto every word. The birth of the Seventh Day Adventist movement is a case in point. William Miller (1782-1849) a Baptist lay preacher founded the Millerite movement who's distinctive was formed around Miller's interpretation of Daniel's prophecies, especially 8:14. Eventually a date was set for the predicted return of Christ—22 October 1844. The day passed as did any other. Naturally there was great disappointment amongst the Millerites. Following that date other days were suggested which also came and went. A new teaching was proposed supporting the prophecy that the world had entered a seventh millennium, called the Great Sabbath. A doctrine quickly developed that said Jesus was now sitting on a white cloud and needed to be prayed down. None of this helped the many disillusioned Millerites who either joined other movements such as the Shakers, returned to their previous denominations or even gave up their beliefs. Still many others would not give up Miller's teaching (and prophecies) so easily and had to find a way through the apparent credibility gap. As a result of the fallout from the Great Disappointment Millerism split into three groups: the 'shut-door' or 'spiritualizer' group, the Advent Christian Church and the Seventh Day Adventist Church.

Therefore, making an obviously wrong prediction did not prevent people from believing it to be true in the face of the obvious and reworking the prophecy to retrospectively fit the circumstances—all that was said prior was conveniently forgotten. The return of Jesus was first re-dated, then spiritualised when that date came and went, so that rather than being an earthly event, the original date was, now in hindsight, deemed correct, with no credibility gap because it was in fact a heavenly event, with the earthly return of Christ still to occur. Heaven had been cleansed—that was what the prophecy was all about—and many swallowed it up. Naturally with this kind of mindset once Ellen G. White started having visions soon after the Great Disappointment she was easily embraced as a great prophet and thus as a great teacher. Her works are preeminent still within Seventh Day Adventism. If we can assume that Miller, Bates, White and other leaders were well-intentioned, they were and are wrong, and one bad prophecy, in this case, does a movement make, and also makes room for much more false prophecy (visions) and thus false teaching. It would appear that particularly the glaring error of the 1844 prophecy being wrong is of little consequence to the now 21 or so million adherents of Seventh Day Adventist doctrine. Clearly being wrong when speaking on behalf of God in the religious mind of many does not matter.

Personal confidence in a person does not a prophet make

Truth is presumably still important, therefore so is accuracy with prophecy, but not so important that it cannot be mitigated if a higher purpose is being served. Spiritualising an event that was supposed to occur on earth is a convenient face saver—and in the heart here, unseen, is malevolence; there can be no purity of heart when this occurs. However, the most likely reason for acceptance of it, is not so much the prophecy per se or its reinvented interpretation, but the trust placed in the prophet themselves. In the church people love prophets in a similar vein as the world loves mystics and mediums. If the prophets are considered to be genuine in terms of their motivation, they live according to the prescribed righteousness of the group with which they are involved, they have an excellent Bible knowledge and they claim to see things that ordinary people do not see, or claim to see; certainly loyalty is given to the prophet which is stronger than the need for the words they give to be 100% accurate. Most words that are given are vague and on the level of Barnum Statements, and as Barnum is quoted as saying, 'A sucker is born every day,' many Christians crave the vagueness of it all.

A number of years ago a man who claimed to be a prophet spoke of a great devastating earthquake to hit the city in which he lived. He put a date on the event and the churches in the region were alerted. The date came and went like Miller's prediction of Christ's return. The prophet then reworked the prophecy with a new date, which also came and went, then he spiritualised the event and the few people who were following him, while acknowledging that the earthquake did not happen, expressed their support for and confidence in the prophet. This support encouraged him to continue and 30 years later he still considers himself to be a prophet of God. He was genuine, expressing how he wants to see God's kingdom on earth and seeks to reinvigorate an unfaithful church. He was essentially a good man and these characteristics were enough to blind his followers into accepting him as a prophet speaking God's words when clearly he was/is not.

Sentiment is the issue here, and sentimentality is the filter for discernment for much of the contemporary church—faith and facts are trumped by feelings; even the clear commands of Scripture. Current issues facing the church such as abortion, gender, feminism and euthanasia, while having clear biblical standards are being re-moralised as many modern Christians use sentiment as their guide and side in sympathy with the people who they consider to be in emotional turmoil as a result of God's clear instruction—God's ways making them miserable, even suicidal. They unwittingly become the enemies of God as they rework biblical interpretation in order to assuage their sentiment. The tendency is to use sentiment as the everyday guide rather than any systematic theological reasoning—concurrent with this is a general biblical illiteracy among many churchgoers. It is the heart that rules and not the head; the soul and not the spirit, just as it is in the world from which the Christian has been supposedly redeemed.

The words must be weighed

As a result it is not the prophetic words that are weighed, rather what is felt about them. Perhaps even more importantly the man or the woman who prophesies is weighed. That might not sound like a bad thing, but sentiment is the filter for weighing—how people feel about the prophets and their words. Truth is somewhere in the shadows only to be brought out as a commodity when needed. People judge or weigh by what they feel in their hearts and not by what they see with their eyes or hear with their ears—though the tone might be weighed more than the words. Of course, what we see of a person superficially as they present publicly is really not an indicator of anything much, but being well practiced at judging a book by its cover, most people feel adept at determining a person's character by the superficial feelings they have—unlike Jesus (cf Isa 11:3). We might say of Eliphaz, Bildad and Zophar that they meant well, and that is what the text indicates, but they spoke wrongly of God—by God's confession. If they were being judged by the contemporary church it is hard to see them receiving any sanction. Sentiment, however, cannot be the church's standard for weighing a prophet (or anything). If a person giving a prophetic word is wrong in what they predict they are not a prophet and should not be listened to or followed (Dt 18:22). Precisely the opposite now occurs among so many in the contemporary church.

The warning that God gave Israel through Moses related to false prophets leading people away from God and His commands. Modern day prophets (some are Christian superstars) might not overtly be leading Christians away from God. The manner in which they come is in Jesus' name, proclaiming Jesus to be the Christ (Mt 24:6). Once said, most Christians put down their guard, as if it is only the people who are claiming themselves to be Christ they should be wary of. This is a proven recipe for deception—every false doctrine of the Roman Catholic church, for instance, has come in this manner, so to that of Seventh Day Adventist teaching as mentioned before: Mormonism, Jehovah's Witnesses, Latter Rain, Jesus only, British Israelism, Dominionism to name just a few. However, left to its natural conclusion modern prophets predicting events and giving words to people that never come to pass and becoming so-called Christian influencers will invariably in time lead people astray (cf Dt 13:1-5). Why? Because though they might sound like they are on the narrow path to the less biblically astute, they are not, and being close to the path is not the same as being on it. Perhaps a word of moderation is needed here—many may have begun by walking on the narrow path and know certain Scriptures well and even lead congregations for some time, but the narrow path is easy to step off if the Christian is not watchful. It would appear, if one wanted to be generous, this is precisely why there are so many false prophets/teachers in the contemporary church—to some degree at least they have stepped off the narrow path while still pronouncing some of its truths. Just as Paul warned the elders of Ephesus that it was from among their own body that false teachers would arise (Ac 20:29-30).

There have been many Christian groups throughout church history that started well, with good intentions, but have not ended well. With the rise of the Charismatic movement this has increased significantly. It is not uncommon for Christians to be involved in parachurch groups gaining teaching and ministry from a teacher(s) who claims a unique connection with the Holy Spirit. There is perhaps nothing superficially untoward with that, small groups have been the mainstay of Christendom since its earliest beginnings. It is the fruit of the ministry that needs to be inspected. Many a small group claiming to be led by the Holy Spirit through an anointed man or woman of God have become dens of iniquity with divorce, adultery, homosexuality being some of the fruit. Job's friends were not of this ilk, but as church history readily provides examples, speaking wrongly of God and His commands is a slippery slope and sentiment as a filtering lens, albeit unconscious, adds much lubrication, and as such true holiness is not a feature of these groups. It is the sense of the leader being 'anointed' by God in some way that has people coming.

All prophets claim a source beyond themselves

A prophet never claims him or herself to be the source of their inspiration. It is a rare thing for a leader in any human sphere to be followed with any fidelity if they do not have something beyond their own person. With prophets of the church they must claim that God, usually by the Holy Spirit, sometimes Jesus or an angel, speaks to them. The basis of Eliphaz's accusations against Job were similar. He claimed that a word came to him via a spirit (4:12-15). The thrust of the message was that if God places no trust in his angelic servants, then how much less with fragile men who might claim a righteousness like God's. 'Placing no trust in', is in the sense of putting no faith or confidence in a person. Job is the obvious target of this word. There is both truth and lie in this message and clearly the spirit that spoke was not a messenger from God. Eliphaz did not make that claim, however, he accepted the word as true and interpreted it in relation to Job's situation, thus concluding that although he had previously acknowledged Job's righteous acts (4:2-6), Job wasn't so righteous after all. No specifics about Job were given but with this spiritual message the seeds of doubt were sown in Eliphaz's mind, so too for Bildad and Zophar. Later they would invent Job's acts of unrighteousness. The effect is to take Job into a deeper despair—consistent with Satan's plan against Job.

Eliphaz never claims more than that a spirit spoke and it was for him a frightening experience. The messenger claimed that God charges angels with error; this can only refer to those who rebelled. He speaks of the destruction of men who perish unnoticed, speaking of not only the fragility of men, but of their inconsequence. Jesus during His ministry makes the point that God has a different perspective in relation to men to the point of counting the hairs of a person's head (Mt 10:29-31); notwithstanding God also sent His Son to die in order for the redemption of individuals. The sense of the inconsequential relevance of men with regard to the gods in Ancient Near Eastern thinking is completely overturned by the New Testament and even though the Old Testament focuses largely on the Israelites, its purview is the world of men and God's redemptive concern. The anti-biblical message given to Eliphaz, which helped form his thinking, led him to speak wrongly about God and thus about Job. To what extent are the modern prophets' claims to have heard from the Holy Spirit accurate? Assuming they are not simply in an emotionally heightened state and are confusing their own thoughts for a message from God by His Spirit, to what extent are they indeed, like Eliphaz, hearing a message from a spiritual being, not in concert with God? Islam and Mormonism both have their foundations in the claim that angels spoke to the prophet and each produced a new testament. Even the author of the *Passion Translation* which has much extrabiblical content, claims to have an angel speaking to him, as well as visits to heaven to discuss issues with holy men long since dead. Alarm bells should be ringing. If a pattern was set with Eliphaz and carried by Bildad and Zophar, something similar must occur today because Jesus spoke of the rise of false prophets, and many are being led astray.

The apostle John's admonition is to test the spirits to see whether they are from God precisely because many false prophets have gone out into the world (1Jn 4:1). Eliphaz, it would appear, made no attempt to question the veracity of what he heard. In hindsight he should have and with the 'many' false prophets at the end of the age no automatic assumption ought to be made that a message received is from God. Every message ought to be tested. Satan is a liar, he would appear as an angel of light, and the purpose of false prophets and false Christs from the devil's perspective is to deceive the elect (Mt 24:24). The church appears to be largely asleep to this. Had Job accepted what Eliphaz had said, he, the elect, would have been deceived. All his friends condemned him as a hopeless case, but by God's grace he would not be dissuaded by their poor theological conclusions and counsel, and their well-meaning motive. Job did not have the word of God with which to defer, only the testimony of his life and a clear conscience. How much more the church has a standard with which to defer when being given messages supposedly to have be sent from above. It would seem though that in dealing with prophetic messages God's word is largely ignored.

Vernon Howell, otherwise known as David Koresh of the Branch Davidians (a Seventh Day Adventist sect) in Waco, Texas proves the point. He prophesied nothing that came to pass as he said. His biblical teaching was wildly errant and many of his followers lapped it up even as it became more outrageous. He had a new interpretation of the Bible and it was this new interpretation for which the people presumably were hungry. They were going to be a part of something—the establishment of God's kingdom from Jerusalem, which never happened, and that teaching also had to be reinvented along with his false interpretation of the fifth seal (Rev 6:9-11). A plain reading of the Gospels alone would have exposed him as a false prophet or wolf in sheep's clothing. Instead of preferring a plain reading of the Scriptures many chose to believe his false prophecy, interpretive lies, bear his children and die an unnecessary horrible fiery death all the while claiming Jesus as Messiah. We do not test the spirits and their messengers and messages to our peril. Jesus has appointed prophets to the church (Eph 4:11), and Peter quoted from Joel on the day of Pentecost that sons and daughters would prophesy (Ac 2:17), but those Scriptures are no basis for accepting a person as prophet simply because they make that claim and tell people things supposedly from God. To do so, and it is claimed, is extreme Christian foolishness. Just as is receiving a message from some well-meaning person with a 'word' and then trying to make sense of it by trying to figure out what it might mean—this is witchcraft. For Eliphaz to claim that a spirit spoke to him, and for the reader of Job to discover that what he said of God was wrong, thus too his conclusions regarding Job means that he acted as medium and not a prophet. How fortunate he was that God was merciful toward him.

Most people have a fascination with the supernatural

People in general have always had a fascination with the supernatural. Christianity attempted to remove the darkness of pagan spiritualism and superstition in light of the revelation of Christ, and superficially within the Christian world and in the life of the church spiritualism of a pagan nature, as in non-Christian, was rejected. For over a millennium little in the way of supernatural occurrences were recorded by the church, notwithstanding that the great institutions of the Western and Eastern Christian traditions had a vested interest in suppressing anything supernatural and leaving it behind with Jesus and His apostles. While not commonplace there was some allowance given but it had to be controlled. During the Second Great Awakening (c. 1800-1850) many spiritual experiences were recorded particularly during the revival tent meetings—this was a time of breaking free from what was considered dead religious Christian institutions. The Second Great Awakening set the stage for the church to reclaim Peter's Pentecost proclamations. The rise of Pentecostalism in the late nineteenth century began to fill the void that was missing in the Christian experience. Today much of Christendom accepts supernatural occurrences such as miraculous healing, prophecy and deliverance from demonic spirits, understood within a biblical framework, though not always practiced within that framework.

The church was birthed with supernatural experience and the miraculous is encouraged in the New Testament, but not without warning and not without admonition to the true motive for the application of spiritual gifts (1Co 13). Jesus also warned that many people who prophesy and perform miracles in His name will not enter the kingdom of heaven (Mt 7:21-23). The warnings are clear, and yet it seems little cognizance is taken regarding them. Alternatively, to take the stance that there is no spiritual gifting of God's people today is equally foolish and denies New Testament teaching. Yet it is not middle ground that we should be after either—rather a biblical path that does not stray into fanciful interpretation but to walk in love (obedience) as Jesus did. All activity is to be in submission to God the Father through His Son, the first call for our agapē love. Clearly Eliphaz, Bildad and Zophar missed the law of love even though they were well-intentioned. Their goal was to help, but when their advice was rebuffed their loving kindness vanished, a very human trait when our good intentions are rejected. Love, as in agapē love, does not respond to rejection in a manner consistent with our fallen nature.

And it is only agapē love as a motivation that has any chance of avoiding the condemnation of Mt 7:23.

Forgiveness is available to those who would speak wrongly for God

However, in saying that, God is merciful. Job's friends, according to God's assessment, deserved punishment. Their perception founded on the words of a spirit (4:15) and conventional wisdom (8:8; 20:4) lead them to judge Job as a sinner receiving due punishment and speak wrongly of God. This was a serious offence in God's eyes. God labels their response to Job and their subsequent misrepresentation of Him as נְבָלָה (*nᵉbēlâ*) very wicked (NIV, NRSV, KJV, NASB folly), which denotes a wicked person rather than merely a person who lacks sense, and is often translated 'disgraceful thing' (cf. Ge 34:7; Dt 22:21; Jos 7:15; Jdg 19:23-24). Following God's command they humbled themselves before Job, who at this point acts as their priest. Job prays for them to which God had promised to respond favourably and the friends are forgiven. Surely God would be merciful to the many false prophets speaking wrongly today if they would come in humble repentance and speak no more. Prophecy is not a game of chance; there is no growing into the prophetic. Either God has given a message as He gave to Samuel as a boy (1Sa 3:2-18), or He has not. Every other word spoken in God's name that is not from God or speaks wrongly of Him is witchcraft and extremely wicked, and repentance is the only course available if such people want to receive forgiveness and not be punished or rejected as their folly deserves.

Eliphaz, Bildad and Zophar become then the first false prophets, false teachers of the Bible. The pattern they set is evidenced in the many false prophets and teachers in the contemporary church. However, unlike Job who was not sentiment based, many of the contemporary church, particularly of the hyper-fundamentalist movements, give ear to false prophets and promote their teaching even when their prophecies are unintelligible or clearly proven to be wrong—their ministries continue. Jesus did say that false prophets would be a feature of the end of the age, and Jesus is proved as a true prophet. However, rather than the desire for false prophets to be thrown into hell for the misleading and worse that they do, the law of love requires some intercession before God's throne of grace that God might have mercy upon them and grant them repentance, so that they might come to a knowledge of the truth and escape the trap of the devil who has ensnared them to do his will (2Ti 2:25-26), just as Eliphaz, Bildad and Zophar had been ensnared so many years before. Job's friends, despite their well-meaning motive, gave comfort in vain as was the devil's intention for Job and is his intention for all God's children.

<h1 style="text-align:center">Select Bibliography</h1>

Barrett, D., & Johnson, T.,   *World Christian Trends AD30-AD2200*, (Pasadena: William Carey Library, 2001).

Boyd-Macmillan, R.,   *Faith That Endures – The Essential Guide to the Persecuted Church*, (Lancaster: Sovereign World, 2006).

Clines, D. J. A.,   'Job', *New International Bible Commentary on CD-ROM*, (Grand Rapids: Zondervan, nd.).

Clines, D. J. A.,   *Word Biblical Commentary: Job 1-20 on CD-ROM*, (Dallas: Word, 2002).

Clines, D. J. A.,   *Word Biblical Commentary: Job 21-37 on CD-ROM*, (Dallas: Word, 2002).

Cosner, L.,   (Dec, 2013). Leviathan — real or symbolic? *Creation.com*. https://creation.com/leviathan-real-or-symbolic

Dobson, J.,   *When God Doesn't Make Sense*, (Wheaton, Illinois: Tyndale, 1993).

Fee, G.D., & Stuart, D.,   *How to Read the Bible Book by Book*, (Grand Rapids: Zondervan, 2002).

Hugenberger G.P.,   'Leviathan', *The International Standard Bible Encyclopedia-Vol 3, K-P*, (Grand Rapids: Eerdmans, 1986) 108-109.

King, M.,   *The Penguin History of New Zealand,* (Auckland: Penguin, 2003).

Lockyer, H.,   'Jemima', *All The Women in the Bible on CD-ROM,* (Grand Rapids: Zondervan, nd.).

Lockyer, H.,   'Keren-Haapuch', *All The Women in the Bible on CD-ROM,* (Grand Rapids: Zondervan, nd.).

Mounce, W. D.,   *Mounce's Complete Expository Dictionary of Old and New Testament Words,* (Grand Rapids: Zondervan, 2006).

Osborne, G. R.,   *The Hermeneutical Spiral,* (Downers Grove, Illinois: IVP, 2006).

Paul, M. J.,   (Dec, 2010). Behemoth and leviathan in the book of Job. *Creation.Com.* https://creation.com/behemoth-and-leviathan

Paul, M. J.,   'Leviathan', *New International Dictionary of Old Testament Theology*

and Exegesis on CD-ROM, (Grand
Rapids: Zondervan, nd.).

Smick, E. B.,   'Job', *Zondervan NIV Bible
Commentary on CD-ROM*, (Grand
Rapids: Zondervan, nd.).

The Boy Prophet
Two Witnesses
The Little Horn
Millennial Reign
Everyone Believes
Epistles in a Nutshell
Salvation…*the things you were probably not told…*

Copies available through:
Author, davidbcaton@gmail.com
Amazon websites